CW00542116

High Protein Raw Food Cookbook

100 Truly Easy and Yummy High Protein Recipes for the Raw Food Lifestyle

Jon Symons

If you have any questions or comments, contact me at jon@jonsymons.com or at my blog JonSymons.com, I'm very happy to hear from you and help out any way I can. You can see all of my books on my Amazon Author page: http://bit.ly/jon-symons-amazon

A Free Thank-you Gift:

I really appreciate your purchase of my book and I'd like to give you another guide that I wrote which is a perfect companion to this book: Easy Small Sprouts (http://bit.ly/sprouting-guide).

It will show you, with full color images, the simple methods I use to grow the healthiest food I know: sprouts. Living sprouts are the pinnacle of raw foods in my opinion, so I hope you'll start adding these low cost, easy to grow, nutritional powerhouse foods to your diet today.

DISCLAIMER

The information in this book reflects the author's opinions and is not intended to replace medical advice.

Before beginning this or any nutritional program, consult your doctor to be sure it is appropriate for you. If you are unsure of any foods or methods mentioned, you should always defer to your physician's advice.

The author has made every effort to supply accurate information in the creation of this book. The author makes no warranty and accepts no responsibility for any loss or damages arising from the use of the contents of this book.

The reader assumes all responsibility for the use of the information in this text.

CONTENTS

Introduction

Part 1 - Where do you Get Your Protein?

As a raw foodie, I get this question, or a variation of it, a lot. Since I've eaten a plant-based raw diet for over four years now, and my health has done nothing but improve during that time, I can say with confidence that I am getting plenty of protein.

But most people have a strong association between meat and other animal products and protein.

As someone who eats a non-traditional diet, I've noticed that "what to eat" is a bit like politics or religion as a subject for conversation. Fun to have a discussion, but the chances of actually changing anyone's mind are very slim.

This book is not attempting to convince anyone on the merits of a plant–based diet, but merely to assure anyone that would like to try raw foods, that getting enough protein is entirely possible, and actually much easier than most people realize.

Before we get into the recipes, I'd like to cover a couple important points regarding protein requirements and how to ensure you're meeting them:

- We actually need less protein than are lead to believe.
- Almost every food has some amount of protein in it.

- Many plant-based foods are very high in protein – even higher than animal protein sources.
- Plant-based protein is easier for the body to extract – digestion is more efficient, which leads to a lighter feeling.

How Much Protein do I Need?

Time for some serious myth busting. According to the USDA the daily recommended requirement for protein is about .36 grams of protein for every pound of body weight. If you weigh 160 pounds, like I do, that's 57.6 grams of protein daily. If you weigh 125 pounds, it's only 45 grams daily.

If you are an athlete, or you are lactating or pregnant, or you are under some other unusual physical or emotional stress, you can increase the multiplier from .36 to .45. Even then, it is still not very much protein that we actually need.

To put those numbers into perspective, one cup of almonds has 30 grams of protein and 1 cup of lentils has almost 20 grams of protein. Now consider that almost every food you eat has some amount of protein in it: fruits, vegetables even a baked potato (a food thought of as a starch, or pure carbohydrate) has 7 grams of protein.

When you start doing the math it's not hard to see that the average American adult consumes over 100 grams of protein a day! We quickly realize that the notion of not getting enough protein is almost certainly a myth.

From a health standpoint, the worst part of this over-consumption of protein is that it is being consumed from unhealthy, high-fat, processed food sources.

Going forward, I invite you, using your weight and any of the other adjustment factors I've mentioned above, to calculate how much protein you really need in a day. Then when you start using the recipes, you can be confident you are getting plenty of this essential nutrient.

Why do We Need Protein?

There is another myth in many people's minds that says we need protein for energy. Just like the idea that we need a lot of protein, this one is also unfounded (the two fallacies actually support each other because people feel tired and run down, then they think they are not getting enough protein).

While it is true that our body will use protein as an energy source, this is only in extreme cases when the body no longer has a supply of carbohydrates or fats. For a person who isn't in an extreme physical situation where they have exhausted all other energy sources in their body, using protein as an energy source would be next to impossible.

It isn't within the purpose of this book to get too

technical, so the short answer for the question of why we need protein is that it is essential for the growth and maintenance of your body tissues.

Proteins that we eat are transformed into many different types of proteins, each with a unique function in the body. Muscles, enzymes, hormones and immune system antibodies are all made by the transformation of the protein we eat.

The reason protein is so essential is that every cell in our body contains protein. As our body manufactures new proteins it replaces dead or damaged proteins in a process of continual growth, replacement and repair.

If we tie all this together, we can understand why weightlifters have the highest protein requirements. They are building massive amounts of new muscle which requires protein. People with challenged immune systems also have higher protein requirements.

As an aside, we start to understand from this brief discussion of how the body uses protein, of why exercise is so important. Periods of strenuous exercise on a regular basis, send signals to our body that we need to get stronger and become healthier. These signals enhance the building and repair mechanisms in the body and our body systems begin to make the improvements happen. Gently pushing your body with regular exercise truly is essential for optimal health.

In the average person's protein requirements are

primarily for maintenance of the body's many systems. That's not to say it isn't important to get enough protein, it is, but it is closer to topping up the oil in your car's engine than it is to filling up your car with gasoline – which is what most of us are lead to believe when it comes to protein requirements.

Protein Content in Foods

- Almost every food has some protein in it.
- Many plant-based foods are very high in protein – even higher than animal protein sources.

Now that we have established the amount of protein we need and how little that amount really is, let's move on to actually figuring out how to ensure we do get enough protein from eating a plant-based diet.

Some examples of protein content in plant foods:

- Lentils – 18 grams of protein per cup
- Chickpeas – 12 grams of protein per cup
- Hemp seeds – 10 grams per 3 tablespoons
- Carrots – 1 gram of protein each
- Quinoa – 9 grams of protein per cup
- Sunflower seeds – 7 grams of protein per 1/4 cup
- Broccoli – 6 grams of protein per cup

There is another way of looking at the protein content in foods and that is by the percentage of the food's total calories that are available as protein.

Here are some examples:

- Sprouts 50%
- Green leafy vegetables 40%
- Bee pollen 35%
- Nuts & Seeds 15%
- Other vegetables 10-40%
- Grains 8-18%
- Fruits 1-7%

Percentage-wise, as a comparison, spinach is about 30% protein and ground beef is about 40%. 100 calories of ground-beef has about 10 grams of protein and 100 calories of spinach has about 12 grams of protein. So in this regard, spinach is the superior choice, right? Well, not so fast, because 100 calories of spinach is *a lot* of spinach for anyone to eat (but not if you're making juice). But the real point here is that spinach and other greens are very viable sources of protein, and if you eat them consistently, along with other high-protein raw foods, as you'll see in the recipes that are found in this book, you won't have any problems getting enough protein.

From the above we can see the surprising protein content in green vegetables. The reason this is important to me is that it gives me a point of caution for anyone embarking on a raw food diet.

"Don't forget the leafy greens!"

There are so many amazing benefits from eating raw food, and as you'll see when you start making the recipes in this book, the food tastes even better than so called "normal" foods. However many people switch to raw food for the health benefits and then skip the leafy greens, which are the most important food anyone can eat.

Raw burgers, delicious dips, crackers and cheesecakes are all amazing but the micro-nutrients found in leafy greens like kale and chard and others are the most important health foods we can put into our body. Deficiencies of these nutrients don't show up in blood tests result in serious illness, but I still believe there is an epidemic of missing nutrients in the standard diet that does show up in fatigue, irritability and depressed mood. I know this from my own experience.

The other reason I like the above list of protein by percentages is that I'm a big sprout eater. (In case you missed it, at the beginning of this book I have linked to a free bonus eBook Easy Small Sprouts (http://bit.ly/sprouting-guide) which will teach you a very simple method for growing sprouts.

What about Complete Proteins?

The last thing we need to cover in a discussion of protein in a raw food or plant-based diet is the concept of complete proteins.

Proteins are actually strands of amino acids, and our body requires twenty different amino acids to properly create protein, but our body is only able to make eleven of these proteins on its own.

This leaves nine amino acids that are commonly referred to as the *essential amino acids*. Essential because it is essential to get them from our diet, because we can't obtain them any other way.

When foods contain all nine of the essential amino acids, they are known as *complete proteins*.

Animal foods are complete proteins, which is why plant-based diets have been seen as inferior when it comes to providing protein.

Unfortunately the complete proteins in animal-flesh foods can also be sources of many other potentially harmful substances like: saturated fats, hormones, cholesterol and many others. And even though they do provide complete proteins, they also lack many substances that are essential for health such as: enzymes, fiber, antioxidants, and phytonutrients.

Let's put aside the discussion of whether of plant-based or animal source food diets are best, and discuss the important question for this book; can someone be healthy and happy and active and thrive on a plant-based diet?

Here's the first important fact... ***many plant foods are complete proteins***. Quinoa, soy products, buckwheat and hemp seeds are all complete proteins! The blue-green algae spirulina is a complete protein that is very easy for the body to synthesize (highly bioavailable) and is 60% protein which is the highest protein content of any natural food.

Many other plant foods are very close to being complete proteins, so that as long as you are eating a variety of these foods, you won't have any problem providing your body with all the raw material amino acids that go into making protein.

More good news is that **you don't even have to eat the foods that combine into a complete protein in the same meal or even on the same day**. Our body can store and combine amino acids, so as long as you are eating a variety of high quality, non-processed, plant-based foods, there is a very little chance you are going to lacking protein.

Here's an example of how easy it is: a simple combination of celery and cucumber (two ingredients that I put into my green juice every day) combine to make a complete protein.

Some other combinations of foods that result in complete proteins:

- Hummus (chick peas and tahini – sesame seeds)
- Any legumes like beans, lentils, and peanuts combined with grains like wheat, rice, and corn
- Lentils and almonds

A brief side note about combining foods. I've written an entire book on the topic (Fart Free Vegan) as I believe it is really important. Some foods like beans (or nuts) and grains don't digest very well if combined in the same meal. It's important to remember that these combinations don't have to be in the same meal, they are just general guidelines to make sure you are getting all aspects of the complete protein profile on a regular basis.

"How Much Protein" Section Summary

In general, the idea of what protein actually does in our body and how much we need is misunderstood.

A lot of people eating a typical diet are probably getting too much protein and from much less than optimal sources.

With a plant based diet is it not difficult at all, with a little bit of knowledge and planning, to get ample protein, even if you are a high-performance athlete or have other circumstances that increase your protein needs.

Most people are surprised to learn that many plant-based foods are actually very high in protein. Again this goes against commonly held beliefs. Sprouts and other leafy green vegetables for example contains surprisingly high amounts of protein.

When it comes to obtaining complete proteins, again it is not difficult with plant-based foods. All that is needed is some awareness of foods that combine to form complete protein. Even without detailed knowledge of amino acid profiles of foods and how they combine, you can almost certainly get complete proteins by eating a variety of organic, raw (or at least minimally processed), plant-based foods.

Part 2 - Soaking Nuts & Seeds

Many people have problems digesting nuts and seeds. Of course some are truly allergic, but in many cases the problem has to do with the natural defense mechanism built into the nuts or seeds.

If we think of a nut or seed in nature, after it falls from its parent plant, and in order to grow into a healthy tree or plant, it may have to endure all manner of circumstances.

For survival purposes, nuts and seeds have developed defense mechanisms which allow them to remain dormant and to only burst back to life when there is enough moisture to give them a chance for long term survival.

These natural defense mechanisms are called enzyme inhibitors. Think of them of a protective coating that prevents enzyme breakdown from taking place. Enzyme breakdown, is what happens when something decomposes. Due to this protective coating found naturally on nuts and seeds, the process of decomposing is minimized so the nut or seed can grow rather than just decaying into fertilizer.

The enzyme inhibitors fight off decomposing bacteria as the nut or seed lay on the ground waiting for enough moisture to trigger its growth.

However when we eat nuts and seeds, our body, in order to extract the nutrients from them, needs to use digestive enzymes in a very similar manner to the decomposition process in nature. This is why eating nuts and sees that still have the protective enzyme inhibitors causes digestive problems for many people.

Soaking and sprouting your nuts and seeds, eliminates the enzyme inhibitors. The nuts and seeds, once soaked in water, naturally shed their protective mechanisms, just as they would laying on the ground when spring arrives, and come to life.

This process of soaking and sprouting makes the proteins and other nutrients in the nuts and seeds more available for our digestive system to extract. It allows us to receive a much greater benefit from these powerful foods.

Grains

Even though they are not used very much as part of this high protein cookbook, unsoaked grains also contain phytic acid which is actually a toxin which works in a similar manner to the enzyme inhibitors in nuts and seeds. This acid can combine with many nutrients in our digestive tract rendering them indigestible.

Consumption of unsoaked grains over the long term can lead to irritable bowel syndrome. Therefore, soaking grains of any kind (wheat, buckwheat, quinoa, spelt, amaranth, millet etc) before eating is also highly recommended.

Soaking Guidelines

Macadamia nuts, Brazil nuts, pine nuts, hemp seeds, pistachio nuts, and hazelnuts do not need to be soaked because the enzyme inhibitors do not exist in these nuts and seeds.

Nut, Seed, Bean or Grain	Soak Time
Almonds	8-12 hours
Brazil Nuts	No Soaking Required
Buckwheat	6-8 hours
Cashews	3 hours
Chickpeas	12 hours
Corn	12 hours
Flax	6-8 hours
Green peas	12 hours
Hemp seeds	No Soaking Required
Kamut	6-8 hours
Lentils	8 hours
Macadamia nuts	No Soaking Required
Millet	8 hours
Pecans	4-6 hours
Pine nuts	No Soaking Required
Pistachios	No Soaking Required
Pumpkin seeds	6-8 hours
Quinoa	4 hours (rinse thoroughly)
Sesame Seeds	6-8 hours
Spelt	6-8 hours
Sunflower seeds	4-6 hours
Walnuts	4 hours
Wheat	6-8 hours
Wild rice	8-10 hours
All other Nuts	6-8 hours

Part 3 - Substitutions

Raw food substitutions play a major role in your raw food kitchen and it's a good idea to have a handy list like this when you go shopping in case you cannot find the right ingredients for your recipes, or don't have time for a separate trip to the health food store.

1 tablespoon hemp oil = 1 tablespoon cold pressed olive oil
1 tablespoon agave nectar = 1 tablespoon honey
1 tablespoon of fresh herbs = ½ tablespoon of dried herbs
1 cup of walnuts = 1 cup of pecans
1 vanilla bean = 1 tablespoon of vanilla extract
1 cup cashews = 1 cup of macadamia nuts
½ teaspoon of cocoa = 1 teaspoon carob powder
1 tablespoon of black sesame seeds = 1 tablespoon white sesame seeds
1 tablespoons Braggs Liquid Aminos= 1 tablespoon soy sauce

Part 4 - Raw Food Kitchen Tools

Setting up your raw food kitchen is require a few tools that will make preparation much easier. Here are seven pieces of equipment you will need.

If you are just starting out, begin with the dehydrator as it is the most essential tool assuming you probably already have some kind of blender.

1. High Quality Blender

The blender is essential for making healthy foods. This piece of equipment helps to turn out smoother, refined sauces, raw nut cheeses, smoothies as well as raw nut milks. The best choice is a powerful high speed blender as they are ideal for most recipes and whole juices.

The most popular brand in raw kitchens is the Vitamix and they are awesome, but expensive blenders. I have also used the Blendtec blender and the Omniblender. The Omniblender is the about $200 less than the Vitamix and the Blendtec, and for all but the most demanding raw chef, will do just fine.

I also recommend having a "Magic Bullet" style small blender. These are super handy when making a quick smoothie for one, for "grinding" some seeds or nuts into "flour" or even making ice cream from a frozen banana. Another great reason for having a mini-blender is that you can take it with you when you travel (just don't take the blade in your carry-on!).

2. Food Processor

Food processors are great for creating pates, shredded salads, desserts and all sorts of puddings too. Processors can be found in smaller sizes which are fantastic if you're only "cooking" for one or two people. Be sure to experiment with the slicer and grater attachments to see what they can do. A big time saver.

3. Juicer

Create delicious drinks by turning fresh vegetables and fruits into juice. The juices can also be used for flavorful raw soup stocks, marinades and sauces. I highly recommend a "masticating" juicer. These juicers process the fruits and vegetables at slower speeds than centrifugal juicers and therefore maintain more of the nutrients and enzymes.

I use an Omega 8006 which I highly recommend. Not only is it a slow speed masticating juicer that makes great juice (and can do nut butters), but it is super fast to clean up which if you use it every day as I do, will save you a lot of time in the long run.

4. Dehydrator

The dehydrator is the foundation of a raw food lifestyle. It is like a stove is to a traditional diet. They are invaluable for dehydrating granolas, seed crackers, vegetables and fruits and they can also heat up foods to give them a slightly softer texture. They're also great for making guilt-free pizzas. When shopping around for a dehydrator, purchase one that comes with Teflex sheets or equivalent non-stick pads that you can lay over the mesh trays – they make dehydrating ultra-simple and the clean-up quick and easy.

I recommend the Excalibur dehydrators. What sets them apart, and you must have this in your dehydrator, is a thermostat. Less expensive units don't allow you to control the temperature, and will likely heat your items to 140° F or more. But to maintain the enzymes and nutritional benefits of raw food never turn your dehydrator above 115° F.

Also get a larger dehydrator than you think you will need. Excalibur sells 4 and 5 tray models as well as the 9 tray version. Get the 9 tray because what happens is that some items you are dehydrating are too tall so you have to remove trays between layers, or you want to dehydrate a bunch of red peppers that you got on sale, and they take a lot of space. For the small extra cost, the larger units are well worth it.

Another dehydrator tip is to keep the unit in your storage room, or even garage. Dehydrators are not super noisy, but they do make some noise, and they often need to run for 12 to 18 hours and any noise can be annoying for that long.

5. Spiralizer

Spiralizers are great fun for creating raw veggie pasta and make preparation quick and easy. You can spiralize cucumber, turnip, zucchini or any mix of your favorites.

Using a spiralizer (here's the one I use and recommend http://bit.ly/spiral-slicer) to make zucchini pasta is so fantastic; you'll never crave wheat pasta again.

6. Kimchi Maker

Kimchi makers are inexpensive items that allow you to make wonderful kimchis and sauerkrauts.
Basically it is just a large glass jar with a water-lock valve that seals out airborne bacteria which could contaminate your krauts, and still lets off pressure that naturally builds up during fermentation. Here is an example for less than $25: http://bit.ly/kimchi-maker

7. Nut bag

A nut bag is useful in a raw kitchen for straining nut milks; separating the pulp from the milk. The advantage of a bag over just using a strainer or sieve is that you can twist the bag, adding pressure, to get every last drop of the precious nut milk. They cost only a couple dollars and will pay for themselves in a few uses.

Section 1: Raw Drinks

RAW MACADAMIA MILK

Total Time: 5 minutes

Servings: 4 (Serving Size: 8 fl.oz.)

Ingredients

- 1 c. raw macadamia nuts
- 4 c. water
- 2 tbsp. raw honey

Directions

1. There is no need to presoak macadamia nuts.

2. In a blender, combine the macadamia nuts and the water. Pulse 3 to 4 times to break up the nuts and then blend at a high speed for about 1 minute or until the nuts are broken into tiny bits.

3. Strain the blended mixture through a fine wire mesh strainer or a nut milk bag. Using a spoon or spatula, help push the milk strain through the nut meal. Then return mixture to the blender and add in the honey; process on medium speed for 30-60 seconds or until the honey is fully incorporated.

4. Place milk in refrigerator to chill. Amount yielded: slightly more than (4) 1 c. servings. The macadamia milk can be stored, covered, in the refrigerator for up to 2 days.

Protein Per Serving: 4g

FERMENTED WATER KEFIR (SODA ALTERNATIVE)

Total Time: 4 -6 days 20 minutes (Includes 4-6 days of fermentation time)

Servings: 4 (Serving Size: 8 fl. oz.)

Ingredients

Water Kefir

- 2 c. water kefir grains
- 2/3 c. organic dark brown sugar (such as sucanat or rapadura)
- 1-2 tsp. organic unsulfured blackstrap molasses
- 1/4 tsp. mineral water (or bicarbonate of soda)
- 20 drops concentrate mineral drops (or other mineral drops or 2 egg shells rinsed and dried out)

Flavoring Additions

- **For Cream Soda** – ½ c. raisins + 1 vanilla bean + another couple drops of bicarbonate of soda (if fizz needed to be increased).
- **For Italian Cream Soda** – Follow the flavor additions for the cream soda, then when the finished cream soda is poured into a glass to serve, add a splash of raw cream (or coconut cream)

- **For Ginger Ale** – 2-4 tbsp. fresh ginger root, grated + ½-1 c. organic raisins (or 4 dates, pitted and chopped)
- **For Lemon/Lime Soda** – juice from 4-6 limes + zest from 1-2 limes, grated

Directions

1. Using a gallon-sized jar with lid, combine the mineral water and sugar. Stir until the sugar is dissolved.

2. Add in the water kefir grains and molasses. Mix well.

3. Seal the lid on the jar tightly. Place the jar in a cupboard ad cover with a towel to block out any light. Allow the water kefir to ferment for a maximum of 24-48 hours or until the water kefir is slightly fizzy and a bit tart.

4. Strain to remove the grains and then place in airtight bottles which have an airlock for a second ferment for the flavoring process.

5. Add your desired flavoring directly into the bottles and allow them to ferment for a maximum of 24-48 more hours. Do not let them ferment for longer or they will turn into alcohol. Also, do not add the flavoring to the first fermentation with the kefir grains. A second ferment has to take place for flavoring only when the water kefir grains have been removed.

6. When the second fermentation is complete, you can transfer to glass soda bottles or place the soda in a glass jar with lid and place in the refrigerator to chill, then serve and enjoy!

Note: Nutritional Data does not include the Flavoring Additions.

Protein Per Serving: 11g

COCONUT-ORANGE JUICE

Total Time: 5 minutes

Servings: 4 (Serving Size: 8 fl. oz.)

Ingredients

- 2 c. coconut water from 2 young Thai coconuts
- 1 c. coconut meat from 1-2 young Thai coconuts
- Juice from 4 oranges, to yield 1 cup
- Juice from half a pineapple, to yield 1 cup

Directions

1. Break open the coconuts and pour the coconut water into a carafe.

2. Peel 4 oranges and remove the skin of the pineapple half; process the oranges and the pineapple through a juicer. Transfer the juice to a blender and add in the coconut meat. Process until smooth.

3. Pour the blended juice mixture into the carafe with the coconut water. Stir to blend. Serve right away or store in the refrigerator for up to 3 days. Yield: 36 fl. oz.

Protein Per Serving: 6g

MANGO LASSI

Total Time: 3 hours 15 minutes (Includes 2-3 hours soaking time)

Servings: 2 (Serving Size: 8 fl. oz.)

Ingredients

- ½ c. cashews, soaked and drained
- 1 med mango, peeled, seeded and diced
- 1 med banana, peeled
- 3 medjool dates
- 3 tsp. fresh-squeezed lemon juice (from 2-3 lemons, depending on size)
- pinch of sea salt, or to taste
- 1 c. water
- 1½ c. ice
- Sprinkle of ground nutmeg (or cardamom, if preferred), to garnish (opt.)

Directions

1. First, presoak the cashews: Place the cashews in a bowl with enough water so that they are fully immersed. Add in 1 tsp. of sea salt per every 2 c. of water to speed up the soaking process. Let the cashews soak for 2-3 hours; change the soaking water once or twice

throughout the soaking time. When the cashews have finished soaking, rinse them thoroughly; drain. Discard the soaking water.

2. In a blender, combine all of the ingredients in the order listed, except for the ground nutmeg (or cardamom). Process until creamy and completely smooth.

3. Pour into glasses and enjoy!

Protein Per Serving:	9g

CREAMY RAW EGG NOG

Total Time: 3 hours 10 minutes (Includes 2-3 hours soaking time)

Servings: 4 (Serving Size: 8 fl. oz.)

Ingredients

- 1 c. cashews, soaked and drained
- 3 c. filtered water
- 5 pitted medjool dates
- 1 medium banana, peeled, sliced and frozen
- ¼ small avocado, peeled, sliced and frozen
- 2½ tsp. vanilla extract
- ⅛ tsp. ground cloves
- 1 tsp. freshly ground nutmeg, plus some to garnish, if desired
- ½ tsp. ground cinnamon
- 4 cinnamon sticks, for garnish

Directions

1. First, presoak the cashews: Place the cashews in a bowl with enough water so that they are fully immersed. Add in 1 tsp. of sea salt per every 2 c. of water to speed up the soaking process. Let the cashews soak for 2-3 hours;

change the soaking water once or twice throughout the soaking time. When the cashews have finished soaking, rinse them thoroughly; drain. Discard the soaking water.

2. While the cashews are soaking, peel the banana and avocado; slice each. Place the slices in a freezer-safe container and place in the freezer for about 1 hour until frozen. Do not remove from the freezer until needed.

3. Place the cashews and water into a blender; process at high for 1 minute.

4. Add in the remaining ingredients; process at high for 1-2 minutes or until smooth and creamy.

5. Pour into 4 8 fl. oz. drinking glasses, garnish each glass with a cinnamon stick. Sprinkle some nutmeg over the surface of the nog, if desired, then serve and enjoy!

Protein Per Serving: 10g

RAW HOT CHOCOLATE

Total Time: 3 hours 10 minutes (Including 2-3 hours soaking time)

Servings: 1 (Serving Size: 8-10 fl.oz.)

Ingredients

- ½ c. cashews, soaked and drained
- 3 medjool dates, pitted
- 3 tsp. cacao powder
- pinch vanilla bean powder
- 1 cup water
- 1 strawberry, to garnish

Directions

1. First, presoak the cashews: Place the cashews in a bowl with enough water so that they are fully immersed. Add in 1 tsp. of sea salt per every 2 c. of water to speed up the soaking process. Let the cashews soak for 2-3 hours; change the soaking water once or twice throughout the soaking time. When the cashews have finished soaking, rinse them thoroughly; drain. Discard the soaking water.

2. Place all of the ingredients, except for the strawberry into a blender; process on high for 1-2 minutes or until smooth and beginning to heat up a bit.

3. Pour into a large mug and garnish with a strawberry, Drink right away and enjoy!

Protein Per Serving: 14g

WARM CINNAMON CACAO

Total Time: 8 hours 15 minutes (Includes 8 hours soaking time)

Servings: 4 (Serving Size: 8 fl. oz.)

Ingredients

Warm Cinnamon Cacao

- 4 c. almond milk (see recipe below)
- 4 - 8 tbsp. cacao, as needed to taste
- 4 tbsp. honey, or more as needed to taste
- ½ -1 tsp. ground cinnamon, as needed to taste

Almond Milk

- 4 c almonds, presoaked and drained
- 16 c. filtered water
- 8 dates
- 4 vanilla beans

Directions

1. First, presoak the almonds: Place the almonds in a bowl with enough water so that they are fully immersed. Add in 1 tsp. of sea salt per every 2 c. of water to speed up the soaking process. Let the almonds soak for 8 hours; change the soaking water once or twice throughout the soaking time. When the almonds

have finished soaking, rinse them thoroughly; drain. Discard the soaking water.

2. ***Prepare the Almond Milk:*** Add the presoaked and drained almonds to a high speed blender or along with the filtered water, dates, and the vanilla bean. Process on high speed for 2 minutes. Strain the blended mixture through a fine wire mesh strainer or a nut milk bag. Using a spoon or spatula, help push the milk strain through the nut meal. Note: you can save the remaining nut pulp and dehydrate it to use as almond flour for other recipes, if desired.

3. ***Prepare the Warm Cinnamon Cacao:*** In the blender, combine 1 c. of the prepared almond milk, 1-2 tbsp. cacao (as needed to taste), honey, and a pinch of cinnamon. Process on high speed until smooth and thickened.

4. Warm the blended mixture to 115°F. If you have a Vitamix blender, you can use the blender to do this or you can very carefully warm in on the stove in a double boiler. If you use the stove, you need to pull the mixture off of the burner, before it reaches 115°F because it will continue to heat even after it is removed from the burner. Use a candy thermometer to monitor temperature and transfer the warm cacao to mugs by the time the thermometer reads 110°F. Serve and enjoy! Yield: A little more than 4 (8 fl. oz.) servings.

Protein Per Serving: 27g

WHIPPED STRAWBERRY-COCONUT SMOOTHIE

Total Time: 10 minutes

Servings: 2 (Serving Size: 8 fl. oz.)

Ingredients

- 4 c. fresh strawberries, hulled
- 2 c. raw coconut milk
- 1 medium pear, chopped
- 1 orange, peeled and sectioned
- 5 to 6 ice cubes
- 4 tbsp. shaved coconut meat, to garnish

Directions

1. Prepare ingredients as directed and then combine the ingredients in the order listed into the blender.

2. Begin blending on low speed and then gradually increase speed to blend on high, continue blending 30-60 seconds or until smooth.

3. Pour smoothie into serving glasses and garnish with shaved pieces of coconut meat. Drink

immediately to receive full nutritional value. Any remaining smoothie can be refrigerated for up 48 hours, in an airtight, opaque container as to not be exposed to light, heat, or air due to risk of oxidation and loss of nutrients.

Protein Per Serving:	8g

FRESH RAW COCONUT MILK

Total Time: 5 minutes

Servings: 4-6 (Serving Size: 8 fl.oz.)

Ingredients

- 1 to 4 mature coconuts (depending on how thick you want your milk)
- 3 cups water

Directions

1. Remove flesh from the coconut(s)
2. Place the coconut flesh in a blender with the water and process for about 3 minutes.
3. Strain through a nut-milk bag.
4. To make the coconut milk even thicker, add the coconut milk just made to the blender along with flesh from another coconut and blend until smooth.
5. Store the coconut in the refrigerator in a glass jar to use as needed. Note: After refrigeration storage, the coconut milk may have some fat collected at the surface. Process it through the blender for a few seconds to reincorporate the fat.

Note: Nutritional Information Based on Using 2 Coconuts

Protein Per Serving: 26g

MINTY-CHIP PROTEIN SHAKE

Total Time: 10 minutes

Servings: 2 (Serving Size: 8 fl. oz.)

Ingredients

- ½ c. full-fat coconut milk
- ½ c. raw coconut meat, chopped
- ½ c. packed raw spinach
- 2 tbsp. packed mint leaves
- 1-2 drops peppermint extract
- 1 c. ice cubes
- 1 avocado, peeled and chopped
- honey, to taste
- 2 tsp. cacao nibs

Directions

1. In a blender, combine the coconut milk, coconut meat, spinach, mint, avocado, and ice until smooth and frothy. Taste and add in the peppermint extract, if needed. Finally, add in the honey and cacao nibs. Blend again very briefly breaking down the nibs into little bits.

2. Pour into 2 glasses, garnish with a sprig of mint and a few chopped cacao nibs. Drink immediately.

Protein Per Serving: 26g

AVOCADO-KEFIR SMOOTHIE WITH MINT & GINGER

Total Time: 5 minutes

Servings: 2 (Serving Size: 8 fl. oz.)

Ingredients

- 1 ripe Hass avocado (to yield approx. 2/3 c. flesh)
- 2 c. plain whole milk kefir
- 1 tsp. fresh ginger, peeled, roughly chopped
- 4 fresh mint leaves

Directions

1. In a blender, combine all of the ingredients into a blender in the order listed and process on high for about 1 minute or until smooth.

2. Pour into 2 glasses and serve immediately to receive full amount of nutrients before they begin to dissipate.

| **Protein Per Serving:** | 11g |

Section 2: Salad Dressings & Sauces

CASHEW PESTO WITH BASIL

Total Time: 3 hour 15 minutes (Includes 3 hours soaking time)

Servings: 4-6 (Serving Size: 1/8 – 1/4 c.)

Ingredients

- 2 c. fresh basil leaves
- ½ c. cold-pressed extra virgin olive oil
- ¾ c. raw cashews, soaked for several hours
- 1-2 large cloves fresh garlic
- 1 handful of fresh watercress or parsley
- juice of one lemon
pinch of sea salt, or to taste

Directions

1. First, presoak the cashews: Place them in a bowl with enough water that they are fully immersed. Add in 1 tsp. of sea salt per every 2 c. of water to speed up the soaking process. Let the cashews soak for 2-3 hours; change the soaking water once or twice throughout the soaking time. When the cashews have finished soaking, rinse them thoroughly; drain. Discard the soaking water.

2. Rinse the basil and watercress (or parsley) and roughly chop.

3. Finely chop 1-2 cloves garlic.

4. Place the soaked cashews, basil, half of the chopped garlic, watercress (or parsley), lemon juice, and a dash of sea salt. Pulse for 30 seconds, then with the motor running, slowly pour in the olive oil and process until the pesto is blended into a thick paste; pausing to scrape down the sides of the blender/food processor jar as needed. Taste the pesto and add the remaining garlic, if needed to taste. Add more sea salt, if needed to taste.

5. Serve the pesto immediately or store in the refrigerator in an airtight container until ready to use.

Protein Per Serving: 9g

GREEN DRAGON DRESSING

Total Time: 20 minutes

Servings: 8 (Serving Size: 1/4 c.)

Ingredients

- 2 ripe avocados
- fresh cilantro, chopped fine to make 1 tbsp.
- fresh parsley, chopped fine to make 1 tbsp.
- 2 tbsp. yellow onion, minced
- The juice of one lime
- 1 jalapeño, chopped fine
- ½ c. extra-virgin olive oil
- ½ tsp. sea salt
- ¼ tsp. fresh ground black pepper

Directions

1. To begin, remove peel from avocados and discard. Prepare remaining ingredients as directed.

2. Combine all ingredients into blender in the order listed. Blend on medium for 15 to 20 seconds or until smooth and creamy or your preferred dressing consistency is reached.

3. Place in a wide-mouthed mason jar with lid or sealable container and refrigerate until ready to serve. Shake or stir well before serving as dressing will separate in refrigerator. Store in sealed container in refrigerator for up to 2 weeks. Yield: 2 cups.

Protein Per Serving:	5g

RAW MAYONNAISE

Total Time: 3 hour 10 minutes (Includes 3 hours soaking time)

Servings: 4-6 (Serving Size: 1/8 – 1/4 c.)

Ingredients

- 1 c. raw cashews, soaked 2 +hours
- ¼ c. water
- ¼ c. fresh-squeezed lemon juice
- 2-3 Medjool dates, pitted
- 1 tsp. sea salt
- 1 tsp. onion powder
- ½ tsp. garlic powder
- ¼ c. extra-virgin olive oil

Directions

1. First, presoak the cashews: Place them in a bowl with enough water that they are emerged. If desired, add in 1 tsp. of sea salt per every 2 c. of water to speed up the soaking process. Let the cashews soak for 2-3 hours; change the soaking water once or twice throughout the soaking time. When the cashews have finished soaking, rinse them thoroughly; drain. Discard the soaking water.

2. In a blender, combine the cashews, water, lemon juice, dates, sea salt, onion powder, and garlic powder. Process until smooth and creamy. With the motor still running, slowly add in the olive oil in a steady stream and process until emulsified.

3. Store in a jar with lid in the refrigerator for up to 2 weeks.

Protein Per Serving: 6g

CHIPOTLE LIME SAUCE

Total Time: 3 hour 10 minutes (Includes 3 hours soaking time)

Servings: 8 (Serving Size: ¼ c.)

Ingredients

- ¾ c. water
- Zest from 1 lime, to yield 2 tsp. grated lime zest
- 1-2 tbsp. fresh-squeezed lime juice (from 1-2 limes, depending on size)
- 1 c. raw cashews, soaked and drained
- ½ tsp. ground cumin
- ½ tsp. chili powder
- ½ tsp. sea salt, or to taste
- ½ tsp. fresh ground black pepper, or to taste
- ½ tsp. chipotle powder

Directions

1. First, presoak the cashews: Place them in a bowl with enough water that they are emerged. If desired, add in 1 tsp. of sea salt per every 2 c. of water to speed up the soaking process. Let the cashews soak for 2-3 hours; change the soaking water once or twice throughout the

soaking time. When the cashews have finished soaking, rinse them thoroughly; drain. Discard the soaking water.

2. In a blender or food processor, combine in this order: the water, grated lime zest, cashews, ground cumin, chili powder, sea salt, black pepper, and chipotle powder. Blend until smooth, creamy, and there is zero grit when you rub the mixture between your thumb and pointer finger. If there is grit, continue processing and continue doing the grit test, until the mixture is smooth when rubbed between your fingertips. Adjust seasonings, if needed, to taste and then process again to fully incorporate any added seasonings.

3. Serve immediately or store in an airtight container in the refrigerator for 5-7 days. Yield: 2 cups.

Protein Per Serving: 6g

THOUSAND ISLAND DRESSING

Total Time: 3 hour 20 minutes (Includes 3 hours soaking time)

Servings: 28 (Serving Size: 2 tbsp. of the dressing)

Ingredients

- 1 c. raw cashews, soaked and drained
- ½ c. sun-dried tomatoes, rehydrated in 3/4 c. of (or more as needed) 115°F warm water
- ¼ c. water
- 5 tbsp. fresh-squeezed lemon juice (from 3-6 lemons, depending on size)
- 2-3 Medjool dates, pitted
- 1 tsp. sea salt
- 1 tsp. onion powder
- ½ tsp. garlic powder
- 2 tbsp. raw apple cider vinegar
- ¼ c. extra-virgin olive oil
- ½ c. red onion, chopped
- ½ c. sweet pickle, chopped

Directions

1. First, presoak the cashews: Place them in a bowl with enough water that they are emerged. If desired, add in 1 tsp. of sea salt per every 2 c. of water to speed up the soaking process. Let the cashews soak for 2-3 hours; change the soaking water once or twice throughout the soaking time. When the cashews have finished

soaking, rinse them thoroughly; drain. Discard the soaking water.

2. Rehydrate the sun-dried tomatoes by placing them in a bowl with ¾ c. of 115°F water. This should be enough warm water so that they are covered; if not, add in more of the warm water until the sun-dried tomatoes are completely submerged and then let them soak in the 115°F water for 10 minutes.

3. Place the cashews in a blender and add in the water, lemon juice, pitted dates, sea salt, onion powder, garlic powder and the apple cider vinegar. Process 1-3 minutes or until smooth and creamy and there is zero grit when you rub the dressing between your thumb and finger. If there is grit, continue processing and continue doing the grit test, until the mixture is smooth when rubbed between your fingertips.   You shouldn't detect any grit. If you do, keep blending till it is creamy smooth when you rub it between your thumb and finger.

4. Next, add in the sun-dried tomatoes along with the water they soaked in; process for 2-5 minutes or until the tomatoes are broken up into tiny flecks. With the motor still running, add in the olive oil in a steady, constant stream until it is completely incorporated. Transfer dressing to a bowl. Finally, stir in the onions and pickle. Serve immediately or store in an airtight container in the refrigerator until needed or for up to 2 weeks. Yield: 3½ cups.

Protein Per Serving: 8g

RANCH DRESSING

Total Time: 3 hour 15 minutes (Includes 3 hours soaking time and 2 hours inactive time)

Servings: 24 (Serving Size: 2 tbsp.)

Ingredients

- 1 c. raw cashews, soaked and drained
- 1 c. water
- ¼ c. fresh-squeezed lemon juice (from 2-3 lemons, depending on size)
- ¼ c. apple cider vinegar
- 2 Medjool dates, soaked in ½ c. of water (Reserve the water)
- ½ c. reserved water from soaking dates
- 2 tbsp. red onion, minced
- 1 tsp. sea salt, or more if needed to taste
- Pinch of fresh ground black pepper, or more if needed to taste
- 3 tsp. onion powder
- 1-2 large cloves garlic, minced (or 1 tsp. garlic powder)
- 1 tbsp. fresh dill (or 1 tsp. dried dill)
- 1 tbsp. fresh basil (or 1 tsp. dried basil)

Directions

1. First, presoak the cashews: Place them in a bowl with enough water that they are emerged. If desired, add in 1 tsp. of sea salt per every 2 c. of water to speed up the soaking process. Let the cashews soak for 2-3 hours; change the soaking water once or twice throughout the soaking time. When the cashews have finished soaking, rinse them thoroughly; drain. Discard the soaking water.

2. Place the dates in a ½ c. water to soak for 10 minutes. Reserve the soaking water.

3. Prepare ingredients as directed.

4. If using as a dip: omit the water. If using as a dressing: include the water

5. *If using dried herbs:* In a blender, add all of the ingredients in the order listed and purée until creamy and smooth.

6. *If using fresh herbs:* In a blender, add all of the ingredients, except for the fresh herbs. Process until smooth and creamy, then add in the fresh herbs and process again until well incorporated.

7. Place the ranch dressing (or dip) in an airtight container and place in the refrigerator to chill for 2 hours to thicken. Then serve when needed. Store any remaining dressing in the airtight container in the refrigerator for 5-7 days. Yield: 3 cups.

Protein Per Serving:	9g

POPPY SEED DRESSING

Total Time: 3 hour 15 minutes (Includes 3 hours soaking time and 2 hours inactive time)

Servings: 24 (Serving Size: 2 tbsp.)

Ingredients

- 2 c. cashews, soaked and drained
- 1 c. pine nuts
- 6 tbsp. extra-virgin olive oil
- 6 tbsp. almond milk
- 1½ c. water
- 6 tbsp. apple cider vinegar
- 6 tbsp. honey
- 6 tbsp. poppy seeds, soaked and drained

Directions

1. First, presoak the cashews: Place them in a bowl with enough water that they are emerged. If desired, add in 1 tsp. of sea salt per every 2 c. of water to speed up the soaking process. Let the cashews soak for 2-3 hours; change the soaking water once or twice throughout the soaking time. When the cashews have finished

soaking, rinse them thoroughly; drain. Discard the soaking water.

2. Meanwhile, soak the poppy seeds for 2 hours in 115°F water, then drain and discard water. Lay the poppy seeds out on paper towel to dry.

3. There is no need to soak the pine nuts as they do not contain enzyme inhibitors.

4. Place all of the ingredients, except for the poppy seeds, in a blender. Process until smooth and creamy. Pour into an airtight sealable jar or containers and stir in the poppy seeds.

5. Serve or store in the airtight container in the refrigerator for up to 5-7 days. Yield: 3 cups.

Protein Per Serving: 11g

Section 3: Chips, Crackers, and Snacks

HONEY GRAHAM CRACKERS

Total Time: 13 hours and 25 minutes (Includes 3 hours soaking time; 10 hours dehydrating time)

Servings: 4 (Serving Size: 4-6 crackers)

Ingredients

- 5 c. cashews, soaked, drained, and ground into a fine cashew flour
- 2 ½ c. raw flaked oats, ground into a fine oat flour
- 1 tsp. sea salt, or more as needed to taste.
- 2 tbsp. ground cinnamon
- ¾ c. water
- 1¾ c. honey
- 2 tbsp. vanilla extract

Directions

1. First, presoak the cashews: Place them in a bowl with enough water that they are emerged. If desired, add in 1 tsp. of sea salt per every 2 c. of water to speed up the soaking process. Let the cashews soak for 2-3 hours; change the soaking water once or twice throughout the soaking time. When the cashews have finished

soaking, rinse them thoroughly; drain. Discard the soaking water.

2. Place the cashews in a food processor and pulse until the cashews are ground into a fine cashew flour. Transfer the cashew flour to a bowl and set aside until needed.

3. Place the raw flaked oats in the food processor and process until a fine oat flour is formed.

4. In a medium-sized mixing bowl, combine the cashew flour, oar flour, salt, and cinnamon. Stir until well combined. Add in the water, honey, and vanilla extract. Mix well with a wooden spoon; you may need to use your hands to blend the contents thoroughly to form a dough-like mixture. Spread the dough mixture out onto non-stick dehydrator sheets until the dough is about 1/8- to 1/4-inch-thick. Score the crackers into preferred shape and size. Dehydrate at 115°F for 4 hours.

5. Once the crackers are dry, transfer them to the mesh dehydrator sheet, place a mesh screen on top of the graham crackers, followed by a dehydrator tray so that the crackers are sandwiched in the center. Flip the tray over, remove the dehydrator tray and remove the non-stick dehydrator sheet. The bottom-side of the crackers should now be facing up. This process will help speed up the drying process. After doing this, dehydrate for an additional 6 hours or until dry and then separate the graham crackers from the scored sheet. You should end up with 16-24 crackers, depending on the size and shape.

6. Serve immediately and store any remaining crackers in an airtight container at room temperature for up 2 weeks.

Protein Per Serving: 30g

HAZELNUT-FIG CRACKERS

Total Time: 20 hours and 15 minutes (Includes 8 hours soaking time; 16-20 hours dehydrating time)

Servings: 4 (Serving Size: 4-5 crackers)

Ingredients

- 1 c. hazelnuts, ground fine in food processor
- 2 c. almonds, ground fine in food processor
- 1 c. raw flaked oats, ground into a fine raw oat flour
- ½ c. ground golden flax
- ½ tsp. ground cinnamon
- 2 tbsp. dried sage
- ¾ c. water
- 2 c. dried figs, chopped fine
- Pinch of sea salt, or to taste
- Pinch of cracked pepper, or to taste

Directions

1. First, presoak the hazelnuts and almonds: Place the hazelnuts and almonds into separate bowls, each bowl containing enough water so that they are fully immersed. Add in 1 tsp. of sea salt per every 2 c. of water to speed up the soaking process. Let the hazelnuts soak for 7-8

hours; let the almonds soak for 8 hours. Be sure to change out the soaking water once or twice throughout the soaking time. When the nuts have finished soaking, rinse them thoroughly; drain. Discard the soaking water.

2. Next, place the hazelnuts and almonds in a food processor and grind into a fine powder (it is okay if a few larger crumbs remain unground). Place the raw flaked oats into the food processor and ground into a fine oat flour.

3. In a large mixing bowl, combine the ground nuts, oat flour, flax, cinnamon, and sage. Mix until well incorporated. Add in the water and then knead into a dough using clean hands. Chop the dried figs and fold them into the dough, kneading, until well incorporated. Roll the dough into a ¼-inch-thick sheet. Cut the sheet into cracker-sized forms (about 1 x 2-inch rectangles or 2 x 2-inch squares). Should yield between 16-20 crackers in total.

4. Place the cracker-shaped dough forms onto the dehydrating screens and place in the dehydrator. Dehydrate at 115°F for 16-20 hours or until the crackers are very dry. Remove from dehydrator and serve or store in a sealable airtight container at room temperature for up to 30 days.

Protein Per Serving: 29g

SPICY CORN "TORTILLA" CHIPS

Total Time: 24 hours and 15 minutes (Includes 8 hours soaking time; 16 hours dehydrating time)

Servings: 4-6 (Serving Size: 10-12 corn chips)

Ingredients

- 6 c. raw corn kernels
- 2 medium red bell pepper, chopped
- 1 small yellow onion, chopped
- 1½ c. flaxseed, finely ground
- 1 c. hemp seed
- 4 tbsp. fresh-squeezed lime juice (from 3-5 limes, depending on size)
- 2-4 jalapeño peppers, minced and seeded (depending on preferred hotness)
- 2 tsp. chili powder
- 2-4 tsp. ground cumin, as needed to taste
- 4 tsp. sea salt, more or less as needed to taste

Directions

1. First, presoak the flax seed (there is no need to soak the hemp seed!): Place the flax seeds into a bowl containing enough water so that the seeds are fully immersed. Add in 1 tsp. of sea

salt per every 2 c. of water to speed up the soaking process. Let the flax seeds soak for 8 hours. Be sure to change out the soaking water once or twice during soaking. Then rinse and drain. Place the flax seeds in a food processor and process until it is finely ground, then transfer to a bowl and set aside until needed.

2. When the flax seeds are finished soaking, add the raw corn, chopped red bell pepper, and chopped yellow onion to a food processor; process until chopped fine.

3. Add ¾ c. of the finely ground flax seed, hemp seed, lime juice, jalapeño, chili powder, ground cumin, and sea salt. Process until the contents turn into a well-blended dough.

4. Using a spatula, spread the dough onto non-stick dehydrator sheets. Score into triangles. Dehydrate at 115°F for 8 hours, then flip sheets over, remove liners, and continue hydrating for 8 more hours or until crisp.

Protein Per Serving: 22g

CINNAMON GLAZED PECANS

Total Time: 18-20 hours 10 minutes (Includes 4-6 hours soaking time; 12-20 hours dehydrating time)

Servings: 8 (Serving Size: ½ c.)

Ingredients

1. 4 c. raw pecans, soaked and drained
2. 4 tbsp. honey
3. 2 tsp. vanilla extract
4. 2 tsp. ground cinnamon
5. ½ tsp of nutmeg, more or less as needed to taste
6. ½ tsp of sea salt, more or less as needed to taste

Directions

1. First, presoak the pecans: Place them in a bowl with enough water that they are emerged. If desired, add in 1 tsp. of sea salt per every 2 c. of water to speed up the soaking process. Let the pecans soak for 4-6 hours; change the soaking water once or twice throughout the soaking time. When the pecans have finished soaking, rinse them thoroughly; drain. Discard the soaking water.

2. Spread the pecans out onto dry paper towel and blot them with the paper towel to dry the pecans before placing in a bowl. Then transfer the dried pecans to a large mixing bowl.

3. Add in with the pecans, the honey, vanilla extract, cinnamon, nutmeg, and sea salt. Toss and stir to coat the pecans well then spread the seasoned pecans onto non-stick dehydrator sheets and dehydrate at 105°F for 12-20 hours or until dry. Note: you can use parchment paper if you do not have non-stick dehydrator sheets, but do NOT use wax paper.

4. Store the pecans in an air-tight container in a cool, dry place for up to 2 weeks. You can adjust the recipe to make a huge batch and then freeze them to be available as needed. Yield: 4 cups.

Protein Per Serving: 6g

CRANBERRY AND WALNUT CRACKERS WITH ORANGE-CRANBERRY SPREAD

Total Time: 18 hours and 45 minutes (Includes 4 hours soaking time; 2 hours marinating time; 12 hours dehydrating time)

Servings: 4 (Serving Size: 4-5 crackers; ½ c. dip)

Ingredients

Cranberry and Walnut Crackers

- 4 c. walnuts, presoaked and drained
- 1 c. ground flax
- 2 c. fresh cranberries, coarsely chopped
- 1 c. fresh-squeezed orange juice (3-5 oranges, depending on size)
- ¼ c. honey

Orange-Cranberry Spread

- Juice from 1 orange
- Zest from 1 orange, grated
- ½ c. flesh from young coconut
- 1 c. cashews, presoaked and drained
- 3 tbsp. honey
- 1 c. fresh cranberries, coarsely chopped

Directions

1. First, presoak the walnuts and cashews: Place the walnuts and cashews in separate bowls, each with enough water so that they are fully immersed. Add in 1 tsp. of sea salt per every 2 c. of water to speed up the soaking process. Let the cashews soak for 2-3 hours; let the walnuts soak for 4 hours. Change the soaking water once or twice throughout the soaking time. When the walnuts and cashews have finished soaking, rinse them thoroughly; drain. Discard the soaking water.

2. ***Prepare the Cranberry and Walnut Crackers:*** Coarsely chop the fresh cranberries and place them into a plastic Ziploc bag with the fresh-squeezed orange juice and the honey. Marinate the cranberries for 2 hours.

3. When the cranberries have finished marinating, place the walnuts in a food processor and pulse until they are finely chopped.

4. Pour the contents of the Ziploc bag (the marinated cranberries, honey, and orange juice) into the food processor with the chopped walnuts and pulse until contents are well blended.

5. Add in the ground flax; pulse until well incorporated.

6. Spread the mixture out into a rectangle about ¼-inch-thick onto a non-stick dehydrator sheet. Score/cut the mixture into cracker shapes, such as 1 x 2-inch rectangles or 2 x 2-inch squares. You should end up with about 16-20 crackers. Dehydrate at 115°F for 3 hours and 45 minutes, then peel off the dehydrator sheets and

continue dehydrating for another 6-8 hours to dry until crackers are done.

7. ***Prepare the Orange-Cranberry Spread:*** Place the fresh cranberries into a food processor and coarsely chop. Transfer the chopped cranberries to a bowl; set aside.

8. Remove the coconut meat from the shell. If there is still brown parts of the shell stick to the back of the coconut meat, take a vegetable peeler, and peel the brown parts off of the coconut meat; discard any remaining pieces of the coconut shell.

9. Place the presoaked cashews, coconut flesh, fresh-squeezed orange juice, orange zest, and honey into the food processor; process until well blended and a good spread-like consistency is reached. Transfer to a bowl and fold in the chopped cranberries. Stir until well incorporated.

10. Yield: 2 cups. Serve 4-5 crackers with ½ c. spread. Store any remaining spread in the refrigerator in an airtight container for up to 5-7 day and store any remaining crackers at room temperature in an airtight container for up to 1-2 weeks. You can also freeze the spread and crackers in airtight, freezer-safe containers for up to several months.

Protein Per Serving: 42g

COCONUT-CHOCOLATE KALE CHIPS

Total Time: 12 hours and 15 minutes (Includes 3 hours soaking time; 6-8 hours dehydrating time)

Servings: 4 (Serving Size: 1 cup)

Ingredients

- 1 c. raw cashews, soaked and drained
- 1 bunch of kale - washed, stems removed
- ½ c. coconut palm sugar
- ½ c. water
- ¼ c. raw cacao powder
- ¼ c. raw cacao butter, melted
- 1 tsp. vanilla extract
- ½ tsp. cinnamon
- ½ c. raw coconut meat, shredded
- ¼ tsp. sea salt

Directions

1. First, presoak the cashews: Place them in a bowl with enough water that they are emerged. If desired, add in 1 tsp. of sea salt per every 2 c. of water to speed up the soaking process. Let the cashews soak for 2-3 hours; change the soaking water once or twice throughout the soaking time. When the cashews have finished

soaking, rinse them thoroughly; drain. Discard the soaking water.

2. To prepare the kale chips, first wash the kale and remove and discard the stems. Using paper towel, squeeze out any excess water. Set the kale aside until needed.

3. In a blender or food processor, begin processing the coconut palm sugar into as fine a powder as possible.

4. In a blender, combine all of the ingredients, except for the cacao butter. Process until smooth.

5. With the motor of the blender still running, gradually add in the cacao butter. Process until combined.

6. Place the kale into a large bowl and then pour the sauce mixture over the kale. Using your hands, work the kale through the sauce to coat evenly.

7. Place the kale on the non-stick dehydrator sheets; spread the kale out across the sheets. Dehydrate the kale at 105°F for 6-8 hours or until dry.

8. Serve immediately or store at room temperature in an airtight glass container until ready to serve. Yield: 4 cups.

Protein Per Serving: 10g

Section 4: Dips & Pâtés

SUNFLOWER-WALNUT PÂTÉ

Total Time: 4 hours 5 minutes (Includes 4 hours soaking time)

Servings: 4-6 (¼ c. per serving)

Ingredients

- 1 c. sunflower seeds, soaked
- 1 c. walnuts, broken into pieces, soaked
- ½ c. celery, chopped fine
- ¼ c. fresh parsley, chopped fine
- ¼ c. sauerkraut, chopped fine and juice to taste (or use pickles, if preferred)
- 2 tbsp. fresh-squeezed lemon juice (from 1-2 large lemons)
- 2 cloves garlic, chopped
- ½ tsp. sea salt
- 2 tbsp. coconut aminos (or Bragg's liquid aminos)
- 1 tsp. apple cider vinegar
- 2 tsp. ground cumin
- 1 tsp. paprika

Directions

1. First, presoak the sunflower seeds and walnuts: Place the sunflower seed and walnuts into

separate bowls, each bowl containing enough water so that they are fully immersed. Add in 1 tsp. of sea salt per every 2 c. of water to speed up the soaking process. Let the sunflower seeds soak for 2 hours; let the walnuts soak for 4 hours. Be sure to change out the soaking water once or twice throughout the soaking time. When the sunflower seeds and walnuts have finished soaking, rinse them thoroughly; drain. Discard the soaking water.

2. In a blender or food processor, combine the presoaked sunflower seeds and walnuts along with the lemon juice, garlic, sea salt, coconut aminos (or Bragg's liquid aminos), ground cumin, paprika, and the apple cider vinegar. Process until smooth. You don't want the consistency too runny or too thick.

3. Transfer the pâté mixture to a bowl and using a wooden spoon, stir in the chopped celery, parsley and sauerkraut (or pickle). Keep stored in the refrigerator in an airtight container until ready to serve. This pâté will stay fresh in the refrigerator for up to 3-4 days.

Protein Per Serving: 14g

WALNUT-HONEY SPREAD

Total Time: 4 hours 10 minutes (Includes 4 hours soaking time)

Servings: 4 (¼ c.)

Ingredients

- 1 c. cashews
- ½ c. pine nuts
- 3 tbsp. raw honey
- 1tsp. fresh-squeezed lemon juice (1 large lemon)
- 1 c. walnuts, chopped

Directions

1. First, chop the walnuts, and then presoak the walnuts and cashews; there is no need to presoak the pine nuts: Place the walnuts and cashews into separate bowls and place enough water in each of the bowls so that the nuts are submerged. Add in 1 tsp. of sea salt per every 2 c. of water to speed up the soaking process. Let the cashews soak for 2-3 hours; let the walnuts soak for 4 hours. Change the soaking water once or twice throughout the soaking time. When the walnuts and cashews have finished

soaking, rinse them thoroughly; drain. Discard the soaking water.

2. Into a food processor, combine the cashews, pine nuts, fresh-squeezed lemon juice, and the honey. Process for 2-4 minutes or until smooth. Transfer the mixture to a bowl.

3. Using a wooden spoon, fold in the chopped walnuts. Serve immediately (this is a delicious spread for crackers) or place in an airtight container and store in the refrigerator until ready to use. The spread will keep fresh in the refrigerator for 3-4 days.

Protein Per Serving: 19g

RAW FERMENTED MANGO SALSA

Total Time: 48-72 hours 15 minutes (Includes fermentation time of 48 hours)

Servings: 8 (Serving Size: ½ c.)

Ingredients

- 2 mangos, chopped
- 2 medium red onion, chopped
- 2 avocados, flesh chopped
- 1 cucumber, diced
- 2 fresh tomato, diced
- 1 red bell pepper diced
- 2 scallions, chopped
- 4 medium sized okra
- 12 green olives, diced
- 12 sugar peas, sliced
- ½ c. apple cider vinegar
- 2 tbsp. raw honey
- 2 tsp. sea salt, or more as needed to taste
- ½ c. extra-virgin olive oil
- One of the following for fermentation:
  - 2 tsp. salt
  - 1-2 tsp. salt and ¼ c. whey
  - 1-2 tsp. salt and ¼ c. water kefir
  - A starter culture such as Caldwell's Cultured Vegetable Starter or Body Ecology Starter Culture and the directed

amount of salt specific to the culture you are working with.

Directions

1. If using a starter culture for fermentation, prepare the culture according to package directions.

2. In a glass bowl, combine the ingredients in the order listed, including the salt, salt + whey, salt + water kefir, or starter cultures. Stir gently with a wooden spoon to blend contents.

3. Place the salsa into a fermentation container and press down, to release some of the excess liquid. You want the vegetables to be immersed under the liquid, so add just as much water as barely needed to cover the vegetables.

4. Ferment the salsa at room temperature for 48-72hours. Once the fermentation process is complete, transfer the salsa to a jar with lid or another airtight container. Serve right away or store in the refrigerator (or root cellar), until needed. Yield: about 2 quarts.

Protein Per Serving: 6g

"CHEESE" DIP WITH SUN-DRIED TOMATOES

Total Time: 10 minutes

Servings: 4 (Serving Size: ½ c.)

Ingredients

- 2 c. macadamia nuts
- Juice from 1 lemon
- 1c. sun-dried tomatoes, softened and chopped
- 3 tsp. dried Italian herb blend of choice
- Pinch of sea salt, or to taste
- Pinch of fresh ground black pepper, or to taste

Directions

1. There is no need to presoak macadamia nuts.

2. Place the macadamia nuts in food processor and pulse until the nuts reach a consistency comparable to ricotta cheese, be sure to not over process. Transfer the macadamia "cheese" to a mixing bowl and gently stir in the lemon juice, softened and chopped sun-dried tomatoes, Italian herb blend, pinch of sea salt, or more as needed to taste, and a pinch of black pepper, or more as needed to taste.

3. Serve with crackers or chips. Store any remaining dip in the refrigerator in an airtight container for up to 3-5 days.

4. Note: If you wish to add a "rind" and shape the dip into a block of "cheese" – shape the mixture into a round form and dehydrate at 115°F for overnight.

Protein Per Serving: 8g

GUACAMOLE DIP

Total Time: 1 hour 10 minutes (Includes 1 hour of inactive time)

Servings: 6 (Serving Size: ½ cup)

Ingredients

- 6 avocados, halved, seeded and peeled
- Juice from 2 limes
- 1 tsp. sea salt, or as needed to taste
- 1 tsp. ground cumin
- 1 tsp. cayenne pepper
- 1 medium onion, diced
- 1 tbsp. fresh cilantro, chopped
- 1 clove garlic, minced

Directions

1. In a large mixing bowl, combine the lime juice and avocado flesh; using a fork or potato masher, mash the avocado and lime until incorporated, then mash in the sea salt, ground cumin, and the cayenne pepper, as well.

2. Using a wooden spoon, fold in the diced onion, chopped cilantro, and minced garlic. Cover the

bowl with plastic wrap and let rest at room temperature for 1 hour, in order for the flavors to meld.

3. Serve immediately. Store any remaining guacamole in the refrigerator in an airtight container for 1-2 days. Yield: 3 cups.

Protein Per Serving: 4g

SPICY CHEESE DIP

Total Time: 3 hours 10 minutes (Includes 3 hours soaking time)

Servings: 4 (Serving Size: ½ cup)

Ingredients

- ½ c. fresh-squeezed lemon juice (from 4-6 lemons, depending on size)
- ½ c. water
- 2 large red bell peppers, seeds removed; roughly chopped
- 2 c. raw cashews, presoaked and drained
- 1 c. nutritional yeast
- 1-2 tbsp. crushed red pepper, or more as needed to taste
- 1-2 tbsp. onion powder, or more as needed to taste
- 4 cloves fresh garlic, minced
- 1-2 tsp. sea salt, or more as needed to taste

Directions

1. First, presoak the cashews: Place them in a bowl with enough water that they are emerged. If desired, add in 1 tsp. of sea salt per every 2

c. of water to speed up the soaking process. Let the cashews soak for 2-3 hours; change the soaking water once or twice throughout the soaking time. When the cashews have finished soaking, rinse them thoroughly; drain. Discard the soaking water.

2. In a blender, combine the roughly chopped red bell pepper, water, and lemon juice. Process until the pepper is liquefied.

3. Add in the presoaked cashews, yeast, crushed red pepper, onion powder, minced garlic, and sea salt. Blend until smooth. Adjust seasonings, if needed, and then process to incorporate any added seasonings.

4. Serve immediately or store in the refrigerator in an airtight container for 5-7 days. Yield 2 cups.

Protein Per Serving: 16g

Section 5: Raw Soups

CORN CHOWDER WITH SUN-DRIED TOMATO

Total Time: 3 hours 25 minutes (Includes 2-3 hours dehydrating time)

Servings: 5 (Serving Size: 2 cups)

Ingredients

- 1 c. cashews, soaked and drained
- 5-6 c. water, divided
- 4 tbsp. raw apple cider vinegar
- 4 tsp. onion powder
- 4 tsp. smoked paprika
- 4 tsp. fresh ground black pepper
- 1 tsp. garlic powder
- 2 tsp. Himalayan or sea salt
- ½ tsp. cayenne pepper
- 4 c. organic corn
- 2 c. Sun-dried Tomatoes
- 4 tbsp. fresh chives
- 4 tsp. dried dill

Directions

1. First, presoak the cashews: Place them in a bowl with enough water that they are emerged. If desired, add in 1 tsp. of sea salt per every 2 c. of water to speed up the soaking process. Let the cashews soak for 2-3 hours; change the

soaking water once or twice throughout the soaking time. When the cashews have finished soaking, rinse them thoroughly; drain. Discard the soaking water.

2. Place the sun-dried tomatoes in a small bowl with enough warm (not hot) water that they are covered. Let them soak in order to rehydrate while you prepare the next part of the recipe. When they are soft, drain the water and chop the sun-dried tomatoes. Set aside until needed.

3. In a blender, combine cashews, apple cider vinegar, 2 c. water, smoked paprika, garlic powder, onion powder, black pepper, sea salt, and cayenne pepper. Process until smooth and creamy without a gritty sand-like feeling when rubbed between your thumb and pointer finger. If this does happen, continue blending until the gritty feeling subsides. Next, add in 2 c. of the corn kernels and the rehydrated, chopped tomatoes (they should be ready now). Process in the blender with the other blended contents until smooth then

4. Pour the blended mixture into a food processor along with the remaining 2 c. corn, chives, dill, and start with 2 c. of water. Process until the newly added ingredients are chunky in texture. Add in up to 1-2 additional cups of water if needed to thin out the chowder.

5. Serve immediately or keep in the refrigerator in an airtight container for up to 4 days. You can also freeze to store larger batches. If you prefer the soup warm, you can place it in your dehydrator at 115°F. for 30-60minutes or until preferred temperature is reached. Tip: It helps a

lot if you heat the soup bowl before adding in the chowder. Yield: 10 cups.

Protein Per Serving: 14g

CREAMY COCONUT AND CASHEW SOUP

Total Time: 3 hours 15minutes (Includes 2-3 hours soaking time)

Servings: 2 (Serving Size: about 2 cups)

Ingredients

- 4 c. water
- 2 c. dried, shredded, unsweetened coconut
- 2 c. raw cashews
- 2 cloves garlic, minced
- 6 dates, pitted and chopped
- Juice from 1 orange
- 1 tsp. onion powder (or 2 green onions, if preferred)
- ¼ to ½ tsp. chili flakes
- 1-2 tsp. sea salt
- fresh basil, chopped *(optional topping)*
- fresh cilantro, chopped *(optional topping)*
- baby spinach, chopped *(optional topping)*
- green onion, whites and/or green parts sliced thin *(optional topping)*
- avocado, sliced *(optional topping)*

Directions

1. First, presoak the cashews: Place them in a bowl with enough water that they are emerged. If desired, add in 1 tsp. of sea salt per every 2 c. of water to speed up the soaking process. Let the cashews soak for 2-3 hours; change the soaking water once or twice throughout the soaking time. When the cashews have finished soaking, rinse them thoroughly; drain. Discard the soaking water.

2. In a blender, combine the water, shredded coconut, cashews, minced garlic, dates, fresh-squeezed orange juice, onion powder (or green onion), chili flakes, and sea salt. Purée until smooth, creamy, and frothy.

3. If desired, add in one or all of the toppings. Serve immediately or store in the refrigerator in an airtight container for up to 5-7 days. Yield: 4 cups.

Protein Per Serving: 32g

AVOCADO-APPLE SOUP

Total Time: 15 minutes

Servings: 4 (Serving Size: 2 cups)

Ingredients

- 2 avocados, chopped
- 4 medium apples, peeled and chopped
- 2 tbsp. white onion chopped
- 4 c. arugula leaves
- 4 tbsp. extra-virgin olive oil
- 4 c. water, for blending
- 2-4 tsp. white onion, minced, to garnish
- Sea salt, to taste
- Fresh ground black pepper, to taste
- Pinch red pepper flakes, or to garnish

Directions

1. First, set aside a few of the arugula leaves, chopped, to garnish.

2. Prepare ingredients as directed.

3. Add to a blender, the avocado, apples, onion, the remaining arugula leaves, olive oil, and the water. Purée until smooth and creamy.

4. Season with sea salt and black pepper, to taste and garnish with the arugula

5. If serving immediately, ladle the soup into 2 bowls. Season with sea salt and pepper, to taste and the garnish with the chopped arugula leaves, finely-minced onion, and a pinch of red pepper flakes, or to taste. Serve! Store any remaining soup in the refrigerator in an airtight container for 3-5 days. If you prefer the soup warm, you can place it in the dehydrator at 115°F. for 30-60minutes or until preferred temperature is reached. Tip: It helps a lot if you heat the soup bowl before adding in the chowder. Yield: 4 cups.

Protein Per Serving: 6g

PISTACHIO & RED PEPPER BISQUE

Total Time: 3 hours 20 minutes (Includes 2-3 hours soaking time)

Servings: 4 (Serving Size: 1½ to 2 cups)

Ingredients

- ¼ c. raw cashews, soaked and drained
- ¼ c. raw pistachios (do not soak)
- 1 medium- ½ of a large ripe avocado, pitted and peeled
- 1 c. unsweetened almond milk (or coconut milk, if preferred)
- 1 c. filtered water
- 1 tsp. fresh-squeezed lemon juice
- 1 shallot, peeled and chopped
- 2 red bell peppers, stemmed, seeded, and chopped
- 1 serrano pepper, stemmed, seeded, and chopped (opt.)
- 2 tsp. sweet paprika
- 1 tsp. sea salt, or as needed to taste
- ½ tsp. ground cumin
- ½ tsp. ground cardamom
- Pinch of fresh ground black pepper, to garnish (opt.)

For the pistou:

- ½ c. packed fresh parsley
- ¼ c. raw pistachios
- 1 tbsp. nutritional yeast
- 1/8 tsp. sea salt, or as needed to taste
- 2 tsp. extra-virgin olive oil

Directions

1. First, presoak the cashews (there is no need to soak the pistachios): Place the cashews in a bowl with enough water that they are emerged. If desired, add in 1 tsp. of sea salt per every 2 c. of water to speed up the soaking process. Let the cashews soak for 2-3 hours; change the soaking water once or twice throughout the soaking time. When the cashews have finished soaking, rinse them thoroughly; drain. Discard the soaking water.

2. ***Prepare the Pistou:*** In a food processor, combine the parsley, pistachios, nutritional yeast, and sea salt; process until contents are roughly chopped. Pour in the olive oil and process again, until the mixture is chopped fine. Transfer to bowl and set aside until needed.

3. ***Prepare the Bisque:*** In a blender, combine the cashews, pistachios, almond milk (or coconut milk), water, lemon juice, chopped shallot, chopped red bell pepper, serrano pepper (if using), paprika, sea salt, ground cumin, and the cardamom. Process until smooth and creamy. Then add in the avocado and blend again.

4. You can serve the soup at room temperature, chilled or warmed to no more than 115°F in the

dehydrator. Before serving, top each serving of soup with one-fourth of the pistou and sprinkle with fresh ground black pepper and additional sea salt, if desired, to taste.

Protein Per Serving: 26g

CREAMY TOMATO BASIL SOUP

Total Time: 20 minutes

Servings: 2 (Serving Size: 2 cups)

Ingredients

- 1-2 c. water
- 1 c. coconut milk (or almond milk, if preferred)
- 2 c. Roma tomatoes, chopped
- ½ c. sun dried tomatoes, soaked in water to rehydrate
- 1 c. celery, chopped
- ¼ c. red bell pepper, chopped
- ¼ c. basil, chopped
- ¼ avocado
- 3 dates, soaked
- 1/8 tsp. cayenne pepper
- Pinch of sea salt, as needed to taste
- Pinch of fresh ground black pepper, to taste
- 2-4 tbsp. raw coconut cream (opt.)

Directions

1. Place the sun-dried tomatoes in a small bowl with enough warm (not hot) water that they are covered. Let them soak in order to rehydrate

while you prepare the next part of the recipe. When they are soft, drain the water and chop the sun-dried tomatoes. Set aside until needed.

2. Next, in a blender, combine 1 c. of water with the remaining ingredients. Process until smooth and creamy. Add additional water, up to 1 cup, if needed for desired consistency.

3. To serve warm, place the soup in the dehydrator at 115°F. for 30-60minutes or until preferred temperature is reached. Tip: It helps a lot if you heat the soup bowl before adding in the soup or you can serve the soup chilled or at room temperature.

4. When ready to serve, ladle the soup into serving bowls, season with sea salt and black pepper, to taste (opt.) and then drizzle a little coconut cream over the surface of the soup, if desired. Then serve and enjoy!

Protein Per Serving: 11g

Section 6: Nutty Salads

AVOCADO-BEET SALAD WITH GINGER-LIME MARINADE AND MACADAMIA CRUMBLED "CHEESE"

Total Time: 15 minutes

Servings: 4 (Serving Size: 1 salad)

Ingredients

Avocado-Beet Salad

- 4 small beets, sliced into thin rounds
- 3 avocados, thinly sliced
- 1½ c. micro greens of choice, tossed in leftover marinade

Ginger-Lime Marinade

- ¼-½ c. extra-virgin olive oil
- Juice from ½-1 lime
- ½ tsp. fresh ginger, grated
- 2 tsp. maple syrup

Macadamia Crumbled "Cheese"

- 1 c. macadamia nuts, chopped
- Juice from ½ of a lime
- 2 tsp. fresh ginger, grated
- 1 tsp. ground cumin
- Pinch of sea salt, or to taste
- Pinch of fresh ground black pepper, or to taste
- 2 scallions, sliced thin

Directions

1. ***Prepare the Macadamia Crumbled "Cheese":***
   There is no need to presoak macadamia nuts. In
   a food processor, combine the chopped
   macadamia nuts, lime juice, ginger, ground
   cumin, and sea salt and black pepper, to taste.
   Pulse until the nuts are finely ground and the
   mixture sticks and holds when pressed together
   with fingers. Stir in the sliced scallions and then
   set aside until needed.

2. ***Prepare the Ginger-Lime Marinade:*** In a bowl,
   whisk together the olive oil, lime juice, ginger, and
   maple syrup; continue whisking until contents are
   well incorporated. Set aside until needed.

3. ***Prepare the Avocado-Beet Salad:*** First, slice the
   beets into thin rounds; thinly slice each avocado.
   Place the sliced beets and avocado into the bowl
   with the marinade; toss to coat and let the beets
   and avocado rest in the marinade for 5 minutes.

4. Next, using tongs or a slotted spoon, remove the
   beets and the avocado from the marinade.
   However, reserve the marinade. Divide the sliced
   beets and avocado among 4 salad plates and
   then arrange the beets/avocado onto each salad
   plate. Throw the micro greens of choice into the
   bowl with the reserve marinade, toss for a few
   seconds to coat, and then top each salad with a ½
   c. of the marinated micro greens. Finally, sprinkle
   the macadamia crumbled "cheese" over each
   salad and serve right away.

Protein Per Serving: 7g

KALE CUMIN SALAD

Total Time: 20 minutes

Servings: 4 (Serving Size: 2 cups)

Ingredients

- 2 bunched kale, washed, stems removed
- 2 tbsp. fresh-squeezed lemon juice
- 1 tbsp. extra-virgin olive oil
- ½ tsp. sea salt
- 4 tbsp. white onion, diced (or red onion, if preferred)
- ½ tsp. ground cumin
- 1/8 tsp. red pepper flakes
- 1-2 c. cherry tomatoes, diced
- 2 avocados, peeled and sliced or diced, to garnish
- 1 c. pine nuts, to garnish

Directions

1. There is no need to soak the pine nuts.
2. In a food processor, combine ½ of the kale and process until the kale s broken up into small bite-sized pieces, but be careful to not over

process and allow the kale to become soup-like.

3. Transfer the kale to a large mixing bowl and repeat the process with the remaining kale. Then transfer that to the mixing bowl as well.

4. Add the salt, lemon juice, and olive oil to the mixing bowl with the kale. Massage the kale with hands to coat. Massage the salt and liquids into the kale.

5. Next, add in the diced onion, ground cumin, red pepper flakes, and diced tomatoes. Stir to mix well.

6. Divide between 4 salad plates and garnish each salad with sliced or diced avocado and ¼ c. pine nuts. Then serve and enjoy!

| **Protein Per Serving:** | 14g |

RAINBOW CHOPPED SALAD

Total Time: 2 hours 30 minutes (Includes 2 hours of soaking time

Servings: 4-5 (Serving Size: 2½-3 cups)

Ingredients

- ½ c. sunflower seeds, soaked and dehydrated
- 1 large had rainbow chard
- 1 large head, purple curly kale
- 2 c. baby Brussels sprouts, shredded
- 2 tbsp. fresh-squeezed lemon juice
- 1 tsp. sea salt
- 2 c. carrot, shredded or chopped
- 2 c. purple cabbage, shredded or chopped
- ½ c. green onions, sliced
- 1 c. yellow bell pepper, diced
- ½ c. celery, sliced
- 1 c. cherry tomatoes, halved if large in size
- 1 tbsp. fresh oregano, minced

Directions

1. First, presoak the sunflower seeds: Place the seeds in a bowl with enough water so that they are fully immersed. Add in 1 tsp. of sea salt per every 2 c. of water to speed up the soaking process. Let the seeds soak for 2 hours;

change the soaking water once or twice throughout the soaking time. When the sunflower seeds have finished soaking, rinse them thoroughly; drain. Discard the soaking water. Place the sunflower seeds in the dehydrator and dehydrate at 115°F until dry and crisp. Set aside until needed.

2. Wash the kale and chard and then remove and discard stems. Using paper towel, squeeze out any excess water. Then chop the kale and chard into small pieces. Transfer to a large mixing bowl.

3. Place the Brussels sprouts into a food processor; process until shredded. Then place in the mixing bowl with the chopped greens along with the lemon juice and sea salt; use your hands to massage the lemon juice and sea salt into the greens.

4. Process remaining ingredients as directed.

5. Next, add in the shredded carrots, cabbage, green onion, yellow bell pepper, celery, sunflower seeds, tomatoes and fresh oregano. Combine well.

6. Divide among salad dishes and serve with dressing of choice. Store any remaining salad in the refrigerator in an airtight container for 3-5 days. Yield: 12-13 cups.

Protein Per Serving: 15g

SPINACH MUSHROOM SALAD WITH MARINADE DRESSING

Total Time: 12 hours 50 minutes (Includes 12 hours soaking time; 15-30 minutes marinating time)

Servings: 4 (Serving Size: 2 cups)

Ingredients

- 2-lbs. raw spinach
- ½ tsp. fine grain sea salt
- Juice of 1 lemon
- 2 tbsp. coconut aminos (or Braggs liquid aminos)
- 4 tbsp. extra-virgin olive oil
- 2 tsp. garlic powder
- ¼ tsp. cayenne pepper, or to taste
- 2 medium tomatoes, diced
- 1 red onion, sliced thin
- 4-6 cups button mushrooms, chopped (quantity dependent on personal preference)
- 2c. cannellini beans, rinsed, soaked and drained
- 1 avocado, diced

Directions

1. First, rinse the cannellini beans and then place them in a bowl of water to where they are covered and soak for at least 12 hours. Then drain, rinse well, and discard soaking water.

2. Wash the spinach and squeeze out any excess water with paper towel. Next, wilt the spinach by placing the spinach in a bowl and adding in the fresh-squeezed lemon juice and sea salt. Using your hands, massage the lemon juice and sea salt into the spinach until it is wilted. Set aside until needed.

3. Prepare the tomato, red onion, mushrooms, and avocado as directed; set aside.

4. Prepare the marinade dressing: In a mixing bowl, combine the coconut aminos (or Braggs liquid aminos), olive oil, garlic powder, and cayenne pepper; whisk until well incorporated.

5. Add the cannellini beans, diced tomato, thinly sliced red onion, chopped mushrooms, and the diced avocado to the marinade. Stir until contents are coated with the marinade and are well combined. Add in the wilted spinach, stirring gently to combine. Let rest at room temperature for 15-30 minutes.

6. Divide between salad dishes and serve! Yield: 8 cups.

Protein Per Serving: 13g

ZUCCHINI PASTA WITH SPICY LEMON PEPPER SALAD

Total Time: 20 minutes

Servings: 2 (Serving Size: 1 salad)

Ingredients

- 2 medium to large zucchini, spiraled/peeled into "noodles"
- 3 c. broccoli florets
- ½ c. sun-dried tomatoes, sliced
- 1 tsp. red pepper flakes
- 2 tsp. fresh lemon juice, or more to taste
- 2-4 tbsp. extra-virgin olive oil
- ½ tsp. sea salt, or more as needed to taste
- Pinch of black pepper, or more as needed to taste
- 1 c. pistachio nuts, chopped, to garnish
- 1-2 tsp. grated lemon zest, to garnish (opt.)

Directions

1. There is no need to presoak the pistachio nuts.

2. Using a spiralizer or potato peeler, create "noodles" from each zucchini. Sprinkle the

zucchini noodles with salt and set aside to soften. However, if you want the zucchini noodles to be a little crunchy, do not add the salt.

3. Next, chop the broccoli florets in to small bite-size pieces. Set aside.

4. Slice the sun-dried tomatoes (You may need to soak them in water for If you don't use oil packed minutes to soften them up if they are hard).

5. In a large mixing bowl, combine the broccoli, sun-dried tomatoes (drained of any liquid), red pepper flakes, lemon juice, olive oil, and the sea salt. Toss to coat well.

6. Next, you can add the zucchini noodles to the mixing bowl and toss to combine with the other ingredients or you can divide the zucchini noodles among

7. Divide the salad between to salad plates and then top the noodles with the broccoli mixture.

8. To serve, garnish each salad with ¼- ½ cup pistachio nuts and grated lemon zest (opt,). Then sprinkle with black pepper, to taste and serve immediately.

Protein Per Serving: 21g

Section 7: Main Meals

Breakfasts

CACAO BUCKWHEAT PUFFED CEREAL

Total Time: 14 hours10 minutes (Includes 4-6 hours soaking time. 8 hours dehydrating time)

Servings: 4 (Serving Size: 1 cup served with ½ c. nut milk of choice)

Ingredients

- 1 c. date paste (see recipe)
- 2 tsp. honey
- ½ c. almond butter, softened
- 3 tbsp. raw cacao powder
- 5 c. sprouted buckwheat
- 1 c. raw cacao nibs
- pinch of sea salt, or more as needed to taste
- 1 c. pecans, soaked and drained, chopped

Date Paste

- 3 c. water
- 2 c. packed Medjool dates
- A pinch or two of sea salt
- Squeeze of lemon juice to help preserve freshness

Directions

1. First, presoak the pecans. Place the pecans in a bowl with enough water to cover them. Add in 1 tsp. salt to expedite the soaking process. Let the pecans soak 4-6 hours. Be sure to change out the soaking water as needed. Then drain, rinse, and discard soaking water. Roughly chop the nuts and set aside.

2. ***Prepare the Date Paste:*** In a blender, combine the water, dates, a pinch of sea salt, and a squeeze or two of lime juice to preserve freshness. Process until completely smooth. Add more salt if needed, to taste and then process again until the added salt is incorporated. Measure out 1 c. for recipe and store any remaining date paste in a sealable container in the refrigerator for 2-4 weeks.

3. ***Prepare the Cereal:*** In a large mixing bowl combine the 1 c. date paste, honey, softened almond butter, and cacao powder. Mix until well blended.

4. Next, stir in the sprouted buckwheat, raw cacao nibs, chopped pecans, and the sea salt; mix until well combined. Add more sea salt, if needed to taste.

5. Spread the mixture onto non-stick dehydrating sheets. Dehydrate at 105°F for 8 hours or until dry.

6. When the mixture is dry, break the dried mixture into bite-sized cereal pieces. Store in a

glass, airtight container or freeze until ready to serve.

7. To serve, place 1 c. of cereal into a bowl and serve with ½ c. nut milk of choice, such as almond milk, coconut milk, macadamia milk, etc.

Protein Per Serving: 9g

RAW SEEDS & BUCKWHEAT CEREAL

Total Time: 12 hours 10 minutes (Includes 12 hours soaking time)

Servings: 1 (Serving Size: 1 bowl; 1 c. nut milk; ½ c. fresh fruit)

Ingredients

- 1 c. buckwheat grouts, hulled
- ¼ c. sunflower seeds, soaked and drained
- ¼ c. pumpkin seeds, soaked and drained
- ¼ c. dehydrated cranberries
- ½ c. raisins
- 2 tbsp. sprout quinoa
- 1 c. water
- ½ c. fresh fruit of choice, to garnish
- 2 tbsp. honey, to serve
- 1 c. raw nut milk of choice, to serve (opt.)

Directions

1. In a mixing bowl, combine the buckwheat grouts, pumpkin seeds, sunflower seeds, quinoa and raisins. Stir to combine and rise well. Add water and cover with plastic wrap and

allow the cereal to soak for 12 hours or overnight.

2. Drain water and transfer the ready-to-eat cereal to a breakfast bowl.

3. Top with your choice of fresh fruit and honey, and then pour in raw nut milk of choice (if using); serve immediately.

Protein Per Serving:	32g

LEMON SCONES WITH BLACKBERRY AND SAGE JAM

Total Time: 9 hours and 20 minutes (Includes 8-9 hours of dehydrating time)

Servings: 8 (Serving Size: 1 scone; 1-2 tbsp. jam)

Ingredients

Lemon Scones

- 2½ c. raw flaked oats, ground into a fine raw oat flour
- 1/3 c. chia seeds
- ½ c. macadamia nuts, finely ground
- ½ c. coconut palm sugar
- Juice of 2 lemons
- Zest of 2 lemons, finely grated
- 1 c. almond milk

Blackberry Jam

- 1 pint (about 1 c.) fresh blackberries
- 1½ tbsp. chia seeds
- 1½ tbsp. dried sage
- 1-2 tbsp. maple syrup

Directions

1. *Prepare the lemon scones:* There is no need to presoak macadamia nuts. Place the macadamia nuts into a food processor and ground into a fine powder (it's okay if some pieces remain unground). Next, grind the raw oat flakes into a very fine oat flour.

2. Ina large mixing bowl, combine the fine oat flour, chia seeds, ground macadamia nuts and coconut palm sugar. Stir well to blend. In a separate bowl, whisk together the lemon juice, lemon zest and almond milk. Set aside for 5 minutes. Then stir the almond milk mixture into the bowl with the dry ingredients; let rest for 5 minutes.

3. Form the scone mixture into flat circle about 1-inch thick and place it on a non-stick dehydrator sheet. Carefully cut the circle into 8 individual wedges and place in the dehydrator. Dehydrate at 115°F or 7-9 hours; separating and removing to a screen half-way through dehydration.

4. *Prepare the Blackberry and Sage Jam:* About 40 minutes before the scones are finished dehydrating, prepare the jam. To do so, place the blackberries, chia seeds, dries sage, and the maple syrup into a blender (or food processor) and process until puréed. Transfer the jam to a bowl, cover with plastic wrap, and let chill in the refrigerator for 25-30 minutes or until set. Serve 1-2 tbsp. of jam with each scone.

| **Protein Per Serving:** | 7g |

ORANGE-GINGER GLAZED RAW DOUGHNUTS

Total Time: 2 hours and 20 minutes (Includes 2 hours of inactive time)

Servings: 10 (Serving Size: 1 doughnut)

Ingredients

Doughnuts

- 4 c. raw flaked oats, ground into a fine raw oat flour
- 2 c. Brazil nuts, ground fine
- ½ c. raw, organic coconut flour
- 2/3 c. honey
- 2/3 c. coconut oil, melted
- ½ c. coconut palm sugar
- 2 tsp. ground cinnamon
- 2 tsp. vanilla extract

Orange-Ginger Glaze

- zest from 2 oranges, freshly grated
- 6 tbsp. freshly-squeezed orange juice (1-2 oranges, depending on size)
- 6 tbsp. raw coconut butter, softened
- 4 tbsp. honey
- 2 tsp. fresh ginger, grated

Directions

1. ***Prepare the raw doughnuts:*** First, there is no need to presoak the Brazil nuts! Place the Brazil nuts into a food processor and ground up the nuts as finely as possible. Transfer to a large mixing bowl. Place the raw flaked oats into the food processor; grind into a very fine raw oat flour. Transfer the raw oat flour to the large bowl containing the ground Brazil nuts.

2. In that same large bowl containing the Brazil nuts and oat flour, also add in the coconut flour, honey, melted coconut oil, coconut palm sugar, cinnamon, and vanilla extract. Stir together until very well blended and a pliable dough forms. Divide the dough into 10 equal pieces and working with one doughnut at a time, press the dough very firmly into a doughnut pan or mold, then tip the pan over and tap to release the doughnut gently so that it maintains the molded form. Lay the raw doughnut onto a large sheet of parchment or wax paper. Repeat process with remaining 9 pieces of dough until you are left with 10 raw doughnut forms lying on the paper.

3. ***Prepare the Orange-Ginger Glaze:*** In a medium-sized mixing bowl, whisk together the fresh-squeezed orange juice, the orange zest, the softened raw coconut butter, honey, and fresh ginger. Whisk until glaze is well incorporated and smooth. Pour the glaze over each doughnut and then let the doughnuts rest at room temperature for about 2 hours or until set. Once set, serve and enjoy or freeze for later use.

Protein Per Serving: 9g

RAW CINNAMON ROLLS WITH ICING

Total Time: 10 hours 40 minutes (Includes 8 hours soaking time; 1 hour 50 minutes dehydrating time)

Servings: 12 (Serving Size: 1 cinnamon roll)

Ingredients

Cinnamon Rolls

- 5 dates
- ¼ c. water
- 1 c. ground flax
- 1¼ c. almond flour
- 1 c. raw flaked oats, grout into a fine oat flour
- 1 c. pecans, chopped fine
- 2 tsp. ground cinnamon
- 3 tbsp. extra-virgin olive oil
- ¼ c. honey
- 1 c. water

Filling

- 1 young Thai coconut (the meat only), roughly chopped
- 1 c. cashews
- ½ c. almonds
- ¼ c. honey
- 1 tbsp. vanilla extract
- ½ c. raisins

Icing

- 1 c. raw cashew butter
- 3 tbsp. maple syrup
- 1 tsp. ground cinnamon
- 1-4 tbsp. water, for desired icing consistency

Directions

1. First, presoak the pecans, cashews, and almonds: Place the pecans, cashews, and almonds into separate bowls, each bowl containing enough water so that they are fully immersed. Add in 1 tsp. of sea salt per every 2 c. of water to speed up the soaking process. Let the pecans soak for 4-6 hours; let the cashews soak for 2-3 hours; let the almonds soak for 8 hours. Be sure to change out the soaking water once or twice throughout the soaking time. When the pecans, cashews, and almonds have finished soaking, rinse them thoroughly; drain. Discard the soaking water.

2. ***Prepare the Cinnamon Rolls:*** First, blend the dates with ¼ c. water to make a smooth paste; set aside until needed.

3. Place the pecans in a food processor, pulse until they are chopped very fine. Transfer them to a large mixing bowl. Next, place the raw flaked oats into the food processor and ground into a fine oat flour. Add that to the bowl with the chopped pecans, along with the ground flax

and almond flour. Mix the contents until well blended.

4. In a separate bowl, combine the date paste mixture, olive oil, honey, and water. Mix until well incorporated, then blend the wet ingredients into the dry flour-pecan mixture. Blend well, then spread the dough out into a rectangle a little less than ½-inch-thick onto a non-stick dehydrator sheet. Dehydrate the dough at 115°F for about 1 hour – 1 hour 15 minutes. Flip onto screen, peel off dehydrator sheet and dehydrate at 115°F for another 20 minutes. While the dough is dehydrating, begin preparing the filling.

5. *Prepare the Filling:* Remove the coconut meat from the shell. If there is still brown parts of the shell stick to the back of the coconut meat, take a vegetable peeler, and peel the brown parts off of the coconut meat; discard any remaining pieces of the coconut shell.

6. Take the presoaked almonds and cashews and place them into a food processor, along with the honey and vanilla extract; process until smooth. Roughly chop the coconut meat. Gently fold the whole raisins and chopped coconut meat into the almond-cashew mixture until thoroughly blended.

7. *Assemble the Cinnamon Rolls:* When the cinnamon roll dough has finished dehydrating, lay the rectangle of dehydrated dough onto a sheet of parchment paper. Spread the filling over the surface of the dough, spreading all the way to the edges on the long sides, but stopping 1- to 2- inches from the edges on the

short sides of the dough. Carefully roll the dough into a log. Then carefully slice the log into individual rolls about 1- to 1½ -inches thick. You should end up with 12 cinnamon rolls. Prepare the icing.

8. ***Prepare the Icing:*** In a small bowl, combine the raw cashew butter, maple syrup, and cinnamon. Mix until well incorporated and then stir in the water 1 tbsp. at a time until desired icing consistency is achieved. Finally, spread the icing over each roll and serve.

Protein Per Serving: 29g

CINNAMON PANCAKES WITH FRUIT TOPPING

Total Time: 8 hours 15 minutes (Includes 8 hours soaking time)

Servings: 2 (Serving Size: 1 fruit-topped cinnamon pancake)

Ingredients

Cinnamon Pancakes

- ¾ c. flax seeds
- 2 bananas
- 1½ tbsp. maple syrup
- 1 tbsp. cinnamon
- 1 tsp. nutmeg
- ½ tsp. allspice
- ½ tsp. cloves

Fruit Topping

- 2 bananas
- ¾ c. fresh mixed berries, of choice
- ¼ tsp. cinnamon
- ¼ tsp. nutmeg

Directions

1. First, presoak the flax seeds. Place the flax seeds in a bowl with enough water to cover the seeds. Add in 1 tsp. of sea salt per every 2 c. of water to speed up the soaking process in each bowl. Let the flax seeds soak for 8 hours. Change the soaking water once or twice throughout the soaking time. When the flax seeds have finished soaking, rinse them thoroughly; drain. Discard the soaking water.

2. Place the flax seeds in a blender or food processor and process until a meal is formed. Transfer the meal to a medium-sized mixing bowl.

3. Place the bananas, maple syrup, cinnamon, nutmeg, allspice, and cloves into a blender; process until smooth and transfer to the bowl with the flax meal. Gently fold the mixture together until well-blended. Let the mixture rest for 5 minutes to thicken.

4. Meanwhile, prepare the fruit topping. To do so, slice the bananas lengthwise into slices that are approximately ¼-inch-thick. Wash the berries under cool running water; dry with paper towel.

5. Next, divide the pancake batter into 2 halves over 2 plates. Using a spatula, smooth the batter into 2 round pancakes. Top the pancakes with the banana slices and then sprinkle with cinnamon and nutmeg. Top the pancakes with mixed berries. To finish, drizzle each pancake with maple syrup and then serve.

Protein Per Serving: 12g

BREAKFAST CRÊPES

Total Time: 17 hours 5 minutes (Includes 8 hours soaking time; 9 hours dehydrating time)

Servings: 2 (Serving Size: 1 crêpe)

Ingredients

The Crepes

- 2 large or 3 small ripe bananas
- 1 tsp. flax seeds, soaked/drained and ground

The Strawberry Jam

- 1 c. fresh strawberries, sliced

The Cream Filling

- 2-3 bananas, peeled, cut into chunks and frozen.

The Fruit Filling:

- ½ c. fresh berries of choice

Directions

1. First, presoak the flax seeds. Place the flax seeds in a bowl covered with water and 1 tsp. sea salt. Let the flax seeds soak for 8 hours. Change the soaking water once or twice throughout the soaking time. When the seeds

have finished soaking, rinse them thoroughly; drain. Place the flax seeds in a food processor or spice grinder and process until ground.

2. ***Prepare the Cream Filling- Part 1:*** While the flax seeds are soaking, peel the bananas for the cream filling and cut each banana into small chunks.

3. Place in a freezer-safe container and place in the freezer. Allow the bananas to freeze and keep them in the freezer until needed.

4. ***Prepare the Crêpes:*** In a food processor, combine the bananas and the ground flax seeds. Process until the mixture forms a smooth liquid. Pour half of the crêpe batter onto a non-stick dehydrator sheet and spread it out with a spatula until it is approximately 1/8-inch-thick and form the shape of a circle – it doesn't have to be a perfect circle, you can fix the edges later. Repeat with the remaining half of the batter on second non-stick dehydrator sheet.

5. Dehydrate at 115°F 3 hours, or until the crêpes are completely smooth to the touch. When the crêpes are finished, remove them from the dehydrator and super, super carefully, begin peeling the dehydrator sheet from the crêpe.

6. Using a lid from a pot, lay the lid on top of each crêpe and trace a perfect circle. Using a very sharp paring knife, cut the circle out of each crêpe. Set aside until needed.

7. ***Prepare the Strawberry Jam:*** Rinse the strawberries under cool running water. Remove the stems and slice the strawberries. Place the

strawberries onto mesh-lined dehydrator sheets and place the strawberries in the dehydrator.

8. Dehydrate at 115°F for 6 hours or until the strawberries are dried out and have become shrunken-looking, but still plump. Remove the strawberries from the dehydrator and place in a food processor. Process until the strawberries form a textured, jam-like appearance. Transfer to a bowl and set aside.

9. **Prepare the Cream Filling- Part 2:** Remove the frozen banana chunks from the freezer, place them in a food processor or blender and process until smooth and resembles soft-serve ice cream.

10. **Assemble the Crêpes:** Lay one crêpe on each of 2 serving plates. Top each crêpe with 1-2 tbsp. of the strawberry jam. Spread 1/3 c. of the cream filling over the jam on each crêpe.

11. Next, sprinkle the cream filling with ½ c. of fresh berries, then fold the crêpe in half and serve immediately!

Protein Per Serving: 8g

RAW PECAN CINNAMON PASTRIES

Total Time: 7 hours 25 minutes (Includes 4-6 hours soaking time)

Servings: 2-4 (Serving Size: 1 cinnamon roll)

Ingredients

- 1 c. dried figs, soaked
- ½ c. pecans, soaked and drained
- 1 tbsp. cinnamon
- ½ tbsp. nutmeg
- 1-2 tbsp. maple syrup,
- ¼ c. pecans, soaked/drained and chopped
- 2-3 tbsp. coconut butter, melted

Directions

1. First, presoak the pecans. Place the pecans in a bowl covered with water and 1 tsp. sea salt. Let the pecans soak for 4-6 hours. Change the soaking water once or twice throughout the soaking time. When the pecans have finished soaking, rinse them thoroughly; drain. Meanwhile, place the figs in a bowl of water as well and lct soak for 30 minutes.

2. ***Prepare the Crust:*** Place the soaked figs in a food processor and process until they are broken up and form a sticky-like dough mixture. Be careful to not over process or the mixture will turn into a paste. Place the fig-dough onto a sheet of parchment paper. Place a 2nd sheet

of parchment paper over the fig dough. Using a rolling pin, roll the mixture out to approximately ¼-inch thickness. Place the parchment-lined fig dough onto a cookie sheet and place in the refrigerator for 10-20 minutes to harden up a bit.

3. ***Prepare the Filling:*** Place the pecans in a food processor; process for about 5 minutes or until an almost nut butter type of mixture is formed, stopping and scraping down the sides as needed. Add in the maple syrup and cinnamon; process to incorporate.

4. Remove the fig crust from the refrigerator and remove the parchment paper. Spread the filling mixture over the crust until the crust is completely covered in an even layer of filling. Sprinkle a few chopped pecans over the filling, if desired. Place the crust back in the refrigerator to set for 10-20 more minutes.

5. ***Complete the Rolls:*** Use the bottom layer of parchment paper to guide the crust up and to get it rolling. Roll it as tightly as possible while still maintaining form. When it is completely rolled, place back in the refrigerator to set for 20 minutes. Then take the log out of the refrigerator and slice into rolls. You should have about 4 rolls. Drizzle the cinnamon rolls with melted coconut butter and the garnish with chopped pecans. Serve and enjoy.

Protein Per Serving: 14g

BANANA PECAN PANCAKES

Total Time: 9 hour 45 minutes (Include 8 hours soaking time and 1-1.5 hours dehydrating time)

Servings: 4 (Serving Size: 3 pancakes)

Ingredients

- 3 c. flax seed, soaked and ground
- 1 c. flax seeds, soaked and leave whole
- 1 c. dried unsweetened coconut
- 1½ c. water
- ½ c. maple syrup
- ½ c. coconut butter, softened
- 2 c. banana, sliced (1-3 bananas, depending on size)
- 1½ c. raw pecans, chopped

Directions

1. First, presoak the pecans and the flax seeds. Place the pecans and the flax seeds in separate bowls; with each bowl containing enough water to submerge the pecans and flax seeds. Add in 1 tsp. of sea salt per every 2 c. of water to speed up the soaking process in each bowl. Let the pecans soak for 4-6 hours; let the flax seeds soak for 8 hours. Change the soaking water once or twice throughout the soaking time. When the pecans and flax seeds have finished soaking, rinse them thoroughly; drain. Discard the soaking water.

2. Place 3 c. of the presoaked flax seeds in a food processor and ground until fine. Leave the remaining 1 c. of soaked flax seeds whole. Next, roughly chop the pecans; set them aside until needed.

3. In a large mixing bowl, combine together the ground flax seed, the whole flax seeds, coconut, water, maple syrup, and softened coconut butter. Stir until well blended into a batter.

4. Using a wooden spoon, gently stir in the sliced bananas. Blend well. Next, fold in the chopped pecans until well incorporated. You may want to use your hands to better incorporate the ingredients.

5. Take about 1/8 – 1/4 c. of dough and shape into a pancake. Place each formed pancake on the dehydrating shelf with screen. You should end up with about 12 pancakes. Dehydrate at 115° for about 1 hour to 1 hour 30 minutes or until set; the pancakes should still be moist however. When the pancakes are finished, place pancakes on each plate and serve. For quick breakfast-on-the-go, double or triple the recipe and freeze a batch of pancakes, lay them out when needed to defrost so that they are ready to grab and go.

Protein Per Serving: 37g

COCONUT YOGURT WITH WALNUTS & GRAPES

Total Time: 4 hours 30 minutes (Includes 4 hours soaking time)

Servings: 2 (Serving Size: 1-1½ c.)

Ingredients

- ½ a bunch of grapes, sliced in half
- ½ c. walnuts, soaked/drained and chopped
- Meat of one coconut
- 1/3 c. of coconut water
- 3 tbsp. maple syrup (or honey)
- Pinch of sea salt

Directions

1. First, presoak the walnuts: Place the walnuts in a bowl with enough water so that they are fully immersed. Add in 1 tsp. of sea salt per every 2 c. of water to speed up the soaking process. Let the walnuts soak for 4 hours; change the soaking water once or twice throughout the soaking time. When the walnuts have finished soaking, rinse them thoroughly; drain. Discard the soaking water.

2. Place the grapes and chopped walnuts in a medium bowl.

3. Place the remaining ingredients in a blender and process until smooth.

4. Pour the yogurt mixture over the grapes and walnuts, toss to coat. Then place in refrigerator to chill for 20 minutes. Then divide between 2 bowls and serve.

Protein Per Serving:	13g

CHIA SEED OATMEAL WITH CINNAMON MIXED BERRIES

Total Time: 30 minutes

Servings: 1 (Serving Size: 1 bowl oatmeal)

Ingredients

- 4 tbsp. of chia seeds
- 1 c. almond milk (or coconut milk)
- 1 tbsp. honey
- ¼ c. unsweetened flaked coconut
- 1 c. mixed fresh raspberries and blackberries
- 1-2 tsp. ground cinnamon

Directions

1. Place the chia seeds in a large serving bowl with the almond milk (or coconut milk). Stir to combine. Add honey, stir again to combine, and then let rest at room temperature for 10-20 minutes or until the chia seeds absorb the liquid and soften and expand.

2. When the chia seed oatmeal is nearly done, place the mixed berries in a separate bowl. Sprinkle the berries with the cinnamon and toss to coat.

3. When the oatmeal is ready, garnish the surface of the oatmeal with flaked coconut and the mixed berries. The serve immediately.

Protein Per Serving: 7g

BREAKFAST TROPICAL FRUIT BOWL

Total Time: 10 minutes

Servings: 2 (Serving Size: ½ c. each fruit; ¼ c. coconut)

Ingredients

- 1 c. papaya, chopped
- 1 c. mango, chopped
- 1 c. pineapple, chopped
- 1 c. banana, chopped
- ½ c. raw coconut meat, chopped fine

Directions

1. Prepare ingredients as directed.
2. Mix all ingredients together in a mixing bowl.
3. Divide between 2 serving bowls and serve immediately.

Protein Per Serving:	12g

LEMON BREAKFAST SCONES

Total Time: 8 hours 15 minutes (Includes 8 hours soaking time; 2-4 hours dehydrating time)

Servings: 2-4 (Serving Size: 2 scones)

Ingredients

- ¾ c. buckwheat, ground
- 3 tbsp. flax seed, soaked/drained and ground into flax meal
- 24 almonds, soaked and drained
- 1 tbsp. lemon zest
- 1 tbsp. fresh-squeezed lemon juice
- ½ c. plus 2 tbsp. almond milk (or coconut milk)
- 1 tbsp. plus 1 tsp. vanilla extract
- 1 tbsp. maple syrup
- 1-2 tsp. poppy seeds

Directions

1. First, presoak the flax seeds and almonds (there is no need to soak the poppy seeds): Place the flax seeds and almonds into separate bowls, each bowl containing enough water so that each are fully immersed. Add in 1 tsp. of sea salt per every 2 c. of water to speed up the soaking process. Let the flax seeds and

almonds each soak for 8 hours. Be sure to change out the soaking water once or twice throughout the soaking time. When the flax seeds and almonds have finished soaking, rinse them thoroughly; drain. Discard the soaking water. Ground the flax seeds into flax meal.

2. Place all of the ingredients in a food processor; process until the dough comes together.

3. Form the dough into scones and place on non-stick dehydrator sheets. Dehydrate at 115°F for 1-2 hours and then flip and continue dehydrating for an additional 1-2 hours. Yield: 4-8 scones.

Protein Per Serving: 18g

BLUEBERRY PANCAKES

Total Time: 11 hours 15 minutes (Includes 8 hours soaking time; and 3 hours dehydrating time)

Servings: 2 (Serving Size: 2 pancakes)

Ingredients

- ½ c. flax seeds, soaked/drained and ground
- 1 c. flax seeds, soaked and drained
- 3 tsp. coconut oil, melted
- ¼ c. honey
- ½ c. water
- 1 c. fresh blueberries
- ¼ c. unsweetened flaked coconut

Directions

1. First, presoak the flax seeds: Place the flax seeds in a bowl containing enough water to submerge the seeds. Add in 1 tsp. of sea salt per every 2 c. of water to speed up the soaking process in each bowl. Let the flax seeds soak for 8 hours. Change the soaking water once or twice throughout the soaking time. When the flax seeds have finished soaking, rinse them thoroughly; drain. Discard the soaking water.

2. Place ½ c. of the flax seeds in a food processor and process until ground. Add in all of the remaining ingredients, except for the blueberries and flaked coconut. Process until smooth. Transfer to a bowl and fold in the blueberries and flaked coconut, until well combined.

3. Form 6-inch pancake circles onto non-stick dehydrator sheets and dehydrate at 115°F for 1 hour 45 minutes, then flip and dehydrate for another 30 minutes to 1 hour or until set. Serve immediately with maple syrup. Yield: 4 (6-inch) pancakes.

| **Protein Per Serving:** | 26g |

APPLE-CINNAMON PANCAKES

Total Time: 14 hours 45 minutes (Includes 10-14 hours soaking time)

Servings: 2 (Serving Size: 1-3 pancakes, depending on size)

Ingredients

- 8 dates, pitted and soaked for 30 minutes.
- ¼ c. of reserved date soaking water
- 1 c. buckwheat groats
- ¼ c. unsweetened shredded coconut
- 1 c. chopped apples, (Fuji or gala)
- ¼ c. maple syrup
- 1 tbsp. vanilla extract
- 1-2 tsp. ground cinnamon, to taste
- 2 tbsp. ground golden flax seed
- Pinch sea salt

Directions

1. Soak the dates in enough water to cover; set aside for at least 30 minutes. Meanwhile, grind the buckwheat groats in a blender or food processor until they are fine crumbs, almost

flour. Set them aside in a separate bowl, add in the shredded coconut; mix well and set aside.

1. In a food processor, combine the remaining ingredients; blend for 20 seconds or until a chunky batter forms.

2. Add the chunky batter to the buckwheat-coconut mixture; stir to combine well.

3. Scoop pancake-size rounds of the mixture onto dehydrator trays. Using a spatula, flatten the pancakes to desired thickness/size (try to get them to be about ½-inch thick, because they will flatten out some more).

4. Dehydrate at 115°F for 6-8 hours, flip them over, remove the dehydrator sheets and then dehydrate for an additional 4-6 hours or until they are a little bouncy/moist to the touch, yet set.. You want them to be a bit squishy still when you press on them with the outsides not too dry. Serve immediately or if needed, store them in the refrigerator in an airtight container for 3-4 days.

Protein Per Serving: 14g

RAW BREAKFAST CEREAL

Total Time: 8 hours 5 minutes (Includes 8 hours soaking time)

Servings: 1 (Serving Size: 1 bowl cereal)

Ingredients

- 1 crisp apple, chopped
- 1 tbsp. raisins
- 1 tbsp. sunflower seeds, soaked and drained
- 1 tbsp. almonds, soaked and drained
- 1 tbsp. buckwheat groats
- 1 tsp. flax seeds, soaked and drained
- ½ tsp. honey
- 1/8 tsp. cinnamon
- 1 c. raw nut milk of choice, chilled.

Directions

1. Presoak the sunflower seeds, almonds, and flax seeds. Place in separate bowls each containing enough water to cover the nuts/seeds. Add 1 tsp. sea salt per 2 c. water. Let the almonds soak for 8 hours, the flax seeds for 8 hours, and the sunflower seeds for 2 hours. Then drain, rinse, and discard water.

2. Chop the apple.

3. In a cereal bowl, combine all of the ingredients, except for the nut milk. Stir to mix. Serve immediately by pouring 1 c. chilled nut milk of choice over the cereal. Serve immediately.

Protein Per Serving: 16g

Lunches

TOMATO SANDWICH WITH ONION BREAD AND CASHEW MAYONNAISE

Total Time: 11 hours 20 minutes (Includes 8 hours soaking time; 3 hours dehydrating time)

Servings: 2 (Serving Size: 1 sandwich)

Ingredients

Onion Bread

- 1 c. flax seeds, soaked/drained and ground
- 1 c. water
- 3 medium onions, sliced thin
- 2 large carrots, grated
- 1 tsp. sea salt
- 3 tbsp. extra-virgin olive oil

Sandwich Fillings

- 1 tomato, slices
- 1 c. lettuce, torn
- ½ white (or red) onion, sliced

Cashew Mayonnaise

- ½ c. cashews, soaked and drained
- ½ tsp. garlic powder
- 1 tsp. honey

Directions

1. First, presoak the flax seeds and cashews: Place the flax seeds and cashews into separate bowls, each bowl containing enough water so that they are fully immersed. Add in 1 tsp. of sea salt per every 2 c. of water to speed up the soaking process. Let the flax seeds soak for 8 hours and the cashews soak for 2-3 hours. Be sure to change out the soaking water once or twice throughout the soaking time. When the nuts/seeds have finished soaking, rinse them thoroughly; drain. Discard the soaking water.

2. Place the flax seeds in a food processor and process until ground.

3. ***Prepare the Onion Bread:*** In a small bowl, combine the ground flax seeds and 1 c. water. Stir to mix, then let rest for 5 minutes to form a gel.

4. Prepare the onion and carrots as directed. Place them in a bowl, add the sea salt and stir to combine.

5. Add in the flax seed gel and stir to blend well. Spread the mixture out onto non-stick dehydrator sheets and place in dehydrator.

6. Dehydrate at 115°F for 1 hour. When the top is slightly dry, flip and dehydrate for 1-2 more hours or until dry (but not hard and brittle).

7. When done, cut the bread into desired sandwich shapes. For instance, cut 2 small English muffin-size forms for your sandwich or cut it into the shape of regular loaf sandwich bread.

8. ***Prepare the Cashew Mayonnaise:*** In a blender, add all of the ingredients. Process until smooth and creamy with a good mayonnaise consistency.

9. ***Assemble the sandwich:*** Prepare the tomato, lettuce, and; onion. Spread the mayo over the onion bread and add the tomato, onion, and lettuce, place the second piece of bread on top to complete the sandwich, then serve right away.

Protein Per Serving:	24g

RAW EGG SALAD

Total Time: 3 hours 10 minutes (Includes 2-3 hours soaking time)

Servings: 2 (Serving Size: 1 c.)

Ingredients

- 1½ c. cashews, soaked and drained
- ¾ c. water
- 1 tbsp. fresh-squeezed lemon juice
- ¾ tsp. turmeric
- 1½ cloves garlic
- ¾ tsp. sea salt, or to taste
- 3 celery stalks, chopped fine
- ¾ c. red bell pepper, chopped fine
- ¾ c. each of any desired addition, such as chopped white onion
- Pinch of fresh ground black pepper, to season
- Pinch of paprika, to season

Directions

1. First, presoak the cashews: Place them in a bowl with enough water that they are emerged. If desired, add in 1 tsp. of sea salt per every 2 c. of water to speed up the soaking process. Let

the cashews soak for 2-3 hours; change the soaking water once or twice throughout the soaking time. When the cashews have finished soaking, rinse them thoroughly; drain. Discard the soaking water.

2. In a blender, combine everything except for the celery and red pepper; process until smooth and sauce-like.

3. Pour yellow "egg salad" sauce into a large mixing bowl, add in the chopped celery, chopped red pepper, and anything else you would like to add, such as chopped white onion, chopped parsley, etc. Mix contents gently with a wooden spoon until well coated.

4. Sprinkle with black pepper and paprika. Serve on a bed of greens or wrap in a romaine lettuce leaf for an egg salad sandwich!

Protein Per Serving: 15g

KALE TABBOULEH WITH FRESH HERBS

Total Time: 15 minutes

Servings: 2-3 (Serving Size: about 2 c. salad)

Ingredients

The Salad

- 2 bunches of parsley, chopped
- 1 bunch kale, stems removed
- ¾ oz. package fresh mint leaves, chopped
- 1½ c. grape tomatoes, halved
- 1 c. cucumber, seeded and diced
- 1 c. hemp seed
- ½ c. sweet onion, diced

The Dressing

- 2/3 c. olive oil
- ½ c. lemon juices
- 2-3 cloves of garlic, minced
- 2 tbsp. sweet onion, chopped
- 1 tsp. sea salt, or to taste
- 1 tsp. thyme
- ½ tsp. fresh ground black pepper, or to taste

Directions

1. There is no need to presoak the hemp seeds.

2. Prepare the salad: First, wash all greens and dry with paper towel, squeezing out excess water. Remove any stems.

3. Shred the kale and place it in a large mixing bowl. Sprinkle on a little sea salt, then using your hands, massage the salt into the kale until it starts to wilt and begins to soften.

4. Chop the parsley and add it to the bowl as well. Chop mint; mix it into the kale-parsley mixture.

5. Add the remaining salad ingredients to the bowl with the greens and toss to combine the salad contents.

6. Prepare the dressing: Place all of the dressing ingredients, except for the olive oil into a blender; process until smooth. With the motor running, gradually add in the olive oil until just barely combined,

7. Divide the salad among salad dishes and drizzle the dressing over the salad. Serve and enjoy!

Protein Per Serving:	32g

RAW CHILI

Total Time: 20 minutes

Servings: 2 (Serving Size: 2 cups)

Ingredients

- 1 large Portobello mushroom cap, chopped
- ½ red bell pepper, chopped
- 2 tbsp. red onion, diced
- 2 large, juicy tomatoes, roughly chopped
- 1 handful of soft, golden raisins
- 1/4 white onion, roughly chopped
- 1 clove of garlic, roughly chopped
- 1-2 dried chipotle peppers, roughly chopped (quantity dependent on preferred spiciness)
- 2 pinches of sea salt, or to taste
- 1 tbsp. chili powder
- 2 tsp. apple cider vinegar
- 1 tsp. ground cumin
- 1 tsp. dried oregano
- 1-2 avocados, sliced, for garnish

Directions

1. Begin by chopping the Portobello cap and the red bell pepper. Add to a mixing bowl. Dice the red onion and add it to the bowl as well.

2. Roughly chop the remaining ingredients and place them in a blender; process until smooth. Pour the mixture into the bowl with the vegetables and stir to blend well.

3. To serve, ladle the chili into serving bowls and garnish with sliced avocado.

Protein Per Serving: 9g

AVOCADO GAZPACHO WITH CUCUMBER

Total Time: 10 minutes

Servings: 1 (Serving Size: 2 cups)

Ingredients

- 1 small avocado
- 1 cucumber, peeled/deseeded, plus sliced cucumber rounds for garnish
- 1 tbsp. onion, minced
- 1 tbsp. extra-virgin olive oil
- 1 tbsp. lemon juice
- 1 tbsp. apple cider vinegar
- ¼ tsp. sea salt
- ¼ tsp. chili powder
- 1 c. water
- Pinch of paprika, to garnish (opt.)
- 6 (¼-inch-thick) raw cucumber rounds, to garnish
- ½ c. pecans, soaked and drained, chopped, to garnish

Directions

1. First, presoak the pecans. Place the pecans in a bowl covered with water and 1 tsp. sea salt. Let the pecans soak for 4-6 hours. Change the soaking water once or twice throughout the

soaking time. When the pecans have finished soaking, rinse them thoroughly; drain. Roughly chop the pecans and set aside.

2. Combine the avocado, cucumber, onion, olive oil, lemon juice, vinegar and water together in a blender.

3. Blend on high speed for 20-30 seconds or until smooth. Sprinkle in the sea salt and chili powder and blend for 5-10 seconds to fully incorporate.

4. Ladle the gazpacho into a serving bowl and garnish with the chopped pecans, raw cucumber rounds and a pinch of paprika (opt.).

Protein Per Serving: 8g

RAW "TUNA" SALAD

Total Time: 12 hours 20 minutes (Includes 8-12 hours of soaking time)

Servings: 2 (Serving Size: 1 salad)

Ingredients

- 1 c. sunflower seeds, soaked and drained
- 1 c. almonds, soaked and drained
- ¾ c. fresh-squeezed lemon juice (from 3-6 lemons, depending on size)
- 1-2 tbsp. water
- ½ c. celery, chopped fine
- ½ c. plus 2 tbsp. red bell pepper, chopped fine
- ½ c. green onion, white and green parts, sliced
- ½ c. plus 2 tbsp. fresh coriander, chopped
- ½ c. plus 2 tbsp. fresh dill chopped
- ¼ tsp. cayenne pepper
- ¼ tsp. garlic powder
- ¼ tsp. chili flakes
- Pinch of sea salt, or to taste
- Pinch of fresh ground black pepper, or to taste

Directions

1. First, presoak the almonds and sunflower seeds: Place sunflower seeds and almonds into separate bowls, each bowl containing enough water so that they are fully immersed. Add in 1 tsp. of sea salt per every 2 c. of water to speed up the soaking process. Let the almonds soak for 8-12 hours; let sunflower seeds for 2 hours. Be sure to change out the soaking water once or twice throughout the soaking time. When the nuts/seeds have finished soaking, rinse them thoroughly; drain. Discard the soaking water.

2. In a food processor, combine the sunflower seeds, almonds, lemon juice, and water; process until a paste is formed. Transfer to a large mixing bowl.

3. Place the chopped celery, ½ c. chopped red bell pepper, sliced green onion, ½ c. chopped coriander, ½ c. chopped dill, cayenne pepper, garlic powder, and chili flakes into the mixing bowl with the paste. Stir to coat the ingredients with the paste. Add in the sea salt and black pepper, to taste.

4. Divide among 2 serving plates; serve over a bed of greens, if desired, then garnish each salad with 1 tbsp. each of the chopped fresh dill, chopped fresh coriander, and chopped red bell pepper then serve and enjoy!

Protein Per Serving: 28g

RAW TORTILLA-STYLE SOUP

Total Time: 15 minutes

Servings: 2 (Serving Size: 2 cups)

Ingredients

- 2 or 3 tomatoes, coarsely chopped
- 1 large red bell pepper, coarsely chopped
- 1 large orange bell pepper, coarsely chopped
- ¼ c. sundried tomatoes, packed
- 2 large stalks celery, coarsely chopped
- ½ c. fresh cilantro, packed
- ¾ c. water
- 1 tbsp. fresh-squeezed lime juice (from 1-2 limes)
- 1 tsp. sea salt, or to taste
- 1 tbsp. ground cumin
- 1 tsp. chili powder
- ½ tsp. paprika
- 2-3 cloves garlic, chopped
- Pinch of cayenne pepper, or to taste
- 1/2 avocado, peeled and chopped

Directions

1. In a blender, combine all of the ingredients, except for the avocado. Process until smooth.

2. Add in the avocado; process again until smooth. Adjust seasonings as needed.

3. To serve, ladle into 2 soup bowls and garnish with some chopped veggies of choice, if desired.

Protein Per Serving: 7g

COLLARD GREEN VEGGIE-NUT WRAPS

Total Time: 12 hours 10 minutes (Includes 8-12 hours soaking time)

Servings: 2-3 (Serving Size: 2 wraps)

Ingredients

Wraps

- 4-6 large collard greens leaves

Veggie-Nut Filling

- ½ c. hazelnuts, soaked and drained
- ½ c. sunflower seeds, soaked and drained
- ½ c. almonds, soaked and drained
- 1-2 sticks celery, chopped
- ½ c. water
- 1 tbsp. extra-virgin olive oil
- 1 tbsp. honey
- 3 tbsp. fresh-squeezed lemon juice
- Pinch of sea salt, or to taste
- 4-6 green onions, to use as ties

Directions

1. First, presoak the almonds, hazelnuts, and sunflower seeds: Place the each nut/seed into separate bowls, each bowl containing enough water so that they are fully immersed. Add in 1 tsp. of sea salt per every 2 c. of water to speed up the soaking process. Let the almonds soak for 8-12 hours; let the sunflower seeds soak for 2 hours; let hazelnuts soak for 8 hours. Be sure to change out the soaking water once or twice throughout the soaking time. When the nuts/seeds have finished soaking, rinse them thoroughly; drain. Discard the soaking water.

2. Combine all of the veggie-nut filling ingredients into a food processor, process until well blended.

3. Layout the collard green leaves.

4. Scoop 2-3 tbsp. of the veggie-nut filling in the center of the collard green and wrap it up sort of like you would a burrito. Tie a green onion around the wrap to hold it together. Serve immediately.

Protein Per Serving: 26g

WALNUT-STUFFED BELL PEPPERS

Total Time: 4 hours 5 minutes (Includes 4 hours soaking time)

Servings: 4 (Serving Size: 1 stuffed bell peppers)

Ingredients

- 8 red bell peppers
- 4 c. walnuts, soaked and drained
- 4 sundried tomatoes, soaked in water for 2-6 hours
- 2 small red onions
- 2 zucchini

Directions

1. First, presoak the walnuts: Place the walnuts in a bowl with enough water so that they are fully immersed. Add in 1 tsp. of sea salt per every 2 c. of water to speed up the soaking process. Let the walnuts soak for 4 hours; change the soaking water once or twice throughout the soaking time. When the walnuts have finished soaking, rinse them thoroughly; drain. Discard the soaking water.

2. Meanwhile, place the sun-dried tomatoes in a bowl of water and let soak to rehydrate for 2-4 hours. Then remove the tomatoes from the water and discard the water.

3. Take 4 of the red bell peppers and slice off the tops, remove the seeds, and chop, then place in a food processor. Add in the walnuts and the sun-dried tomatoes. Process until the mixture forms a pâté-like mixture. Transfer the mixture to a bowl.

4. Next, finely chop the onion and stir it into the pâté mixture until just combined.

5. Take the 4 remaining red bell peppers, and slice off the tops, but reserve them. Scoop out the seeds and discard. Spoon the pâté mixture into each pepper to fill and then replace the tops of the peppers.

6. Slice the zucchini into spiraled slices, place the spiral slices around the peppers on the serving plates. Serve alongside some finely sliced sundried tomatoes, fresh coriander leaves, and some walnuts. Drizzle some olive oil over the zucchini and serve.

| **Protein Per Serving:** | 24g |

RAW MACARONI & CHEESE

Total Time: 5 hours 25 minutes (Includes 2-3 hours soaking time; 1-2 hours dehydrating time)

Servings: 4 (Serving Size: 2 cups)

Ingredients

Noodles

- 3-4 zucchini

Sauce

- 1 c. cashews, soaked and drained
- 1/3 c. red bell pepper, chopped
- ¼ c. water
- 4 tsp. fresh-squeezed lemon juice
- 3 tbsp. extra-virgin olive oil
- 3 tbsp. nutritional yeast
- ½ tsp. sea salt, or to taste
- ½ very small clove garlic, minced
- ¼ tsp. onion powder
- ¼ tsp. apple cider vinegar

Topping

- 1 c. walnuts, soaked/drained and chopped
- pinch of sea salt, or to taste
- pinch of fresh ground black pepper, or to taste (opt.)

Directions

1. First, presoak the cashews and walnuts: Place the cashews and walnuts in separate bowls with enough water so that they are fully immersed. Add in 1 tsp. of sea salt per every 2 c. of water to speed up the soaking process. Let the cashews soak for 3-4 hours; let the walnuts soak for 4 hours; change the soaking water once or twice throughout the soaking time. When the cashews and walnuts have finished soaking, rinse them thoroughly; drain. Discard the soaking water.

2. *Prepare the Noodles:* Slice the zucchini into long strips with a vegetable peeler, then stack the strips and slice into noodle-like pieces. Place the noodles in a large bowl. Set aside until needed.

3. *Prepare the Sauce:* In a blender, combine all of the sauce ingredients. Process until smooth.

4. Pour the sauce over the zucchini noodles and toss well to coat. Spread the coated noodles and sauce into a shallow dish.

5. Sprinkle chopped walnuts, sea salt, and black pepper (if using) over the surface of the macaroni and cheese dish and then place in the dehydrator. Dehydrate at 115°F for 1-2 hours. Then serve.

Protein Per Serving: 18g

SPRING ROLLS WITH CHILE SAUCE

Total Time: 15 minutes

Servings: 4 (Serving Size: 6 slices, ¼ c. sauce)

Ingredients

- 2 c. romaine lettuce, torn
- 2 carrots, shredded
- 2 c. red cabbage, shredded
- 1 cucumber, shredded
- 1-2 avocados, sliced
- 4 raw nori sheets

Chili Sauce

- ¼ c. honey
- ¼ c. filtered water
- 1 tbsp. red chili pepper
- 1 tsp. sea salt, or to taste
- ¼ turnip, sliced
- ½ of a carrot, shredded

Directions

1. Prepare the sauce: In a blender, combine all of the sauce ingredients (The sauce is spicy so begin with ¼ of a slice of turnip). Process until smooth.

2. Lay the raw nori sheets on a flat surface. Top the each sheet with the torn romaine lettuce and then top with the avocado, carrots, and red cabbage. Roll tight and slice. Each roll should yield 6 slices for a total of 24 slices. Place 6 slices on each plate and serve with ¼ c. chili sauce.

Protein Per Serving: 6g

CUCUMBER SANDWICH ON "RYE BREAD" WITH CASHEW CREAM CHEESE

Total Time: 24 hours 5 minutes (Includes 8 hours soaking time; 12-16 hours dehydrating time)

Servings: 2-3 (Serving Size: 1 sandwich)

Ingredients

Rye Bread

- 3 c. sunflower seeds, soaked and drained
- ¾ c. flax seeds, soaked and drained
- ¼ c. water
- 3 tbsp. caraway seeds
- 2 tsp. sea salt
- ½ c. fresh-squeezed lemon juice
- ¼ c. extra-virgin olive oil

Cashew Cream Cheese

- 1½ c. cashews, soaked and drained
- juice from 2 lemons
- ¼ tsp. sea salt, or to taste
- 2-3 cloves garlic, minced
- Fresh basil, chopped fine, to taste
- Fresh parsley, chopped fine, to taste

Sandwich Fillings

- 1 cucumber, sliced
- Fresh sprouts of choice, if desired

Directions

1. First, presoak the sunflower seeds, flax seeds, and cashews: Place the sunflower seeds, flax seeds, and cashews into separate bowls, each bowl containing enough water so that they are fully immersed. Add in 1 tsp. of sea salt per every 2 c. of water to speed up the soaking process. Let the flax seeds soak for 8 hours; let the cashews soak for 2-3 hours; let the sunflower seeds soak for 2 hours. Be sure to change out the soaking water once or twice throughout the soaking time. When the nuts/seeds have finished soaking, rinse them thoroughly; drain. Discard the soaking water.

2. ***Prepare the "Rye Bread":*** Place the caraway seeds and flax seeds in a food processor or spice/coffee grinder and ground into a fine mixture. Place all of the rye bread ingredients into the food processor; process until well blended. Spread the dough out onto non-stick dehydrating sheets. Dehydrate at 105°F for 12-16 hours, flipping the bread half way through.

3. ***Prepare the Cashew Cream Cheese:*** In a food processor, combine the cashews, lemon juice, and sea salt. Process until well blended, then gently add in the chopped garlic, parsley, and basil and pulse until gently incorporated.

4. Cut the sheets of bread dough into slices of bread. Spread the cream cheese over the bread and top with sliced cucumber and fresh sprouts (if using), then top with 2nd piece of bread to complete. Serve immediately.

Protein Per Serving: 48g

PARSNIP RICE WITH HEMP SEED AND BASIL

Total Time: 10 minutes

Servings: 2 (Serving Size: 2 cups)

Ingredients

- 1 lb. parsnips, peeled and roughly chopped
- 2 tbsp. hemp seeds
- ¼ tsp. sea salt, or to taste
- Dash of black pepper, or to taste
- 1 tbsp. hemp oil (or olive or avocado oil)
- Juice from ½ a lemon
- ¼ c. fresh basil, chopped

Directions

1. There is no need to presoak the hemp seeds.

2. Place parsnips, hemp seeds, sea salt, and pepper in a food processor. Process till the mixture is finely chopped, and resembles rice.

3. Transfer parsnip mixture to a bowl and toss to combine with the hemp oil, lemon, and basil. Then transfer to serving bowls and serve.

| **Protein Per Serving:** | 16g |

CHIA QUINOA KHEER (INDIAN RICE PUDDING)

Total Time: 32 hours, 15 minutes (Includes 8 hours soaking time; 24 hours sprouting time)

Servings: 1 (Serving Size: 2 cups)

Ingredients

- 1 1/3 c. quinoa, soaked to sprout
- 3-5 c. cool water
- 3 tbsp. honey
- 1 tbsp. chia seeds
- ½ tsp. vanilla extract
- 3 tbsp. almonds, soaked/drained and chopped
- 3 tbsp. pistachios, chopped
- ½ tsp. ground nutmeg
- ¾ tsp. cinnamon
- ¼ c. raisins
- Coconut cream (or almond cream), for serving

Directions

1. First, sprout the Quinoa: For 2 cups of sprout quinoa, place 11/3 c. quinoa in a jar and add 2-3 times that in cool water, stir to combine. Soak

for 30 minutes. Drain the soaking water, rinse the quinoa well and drain. Place a mesh lid or cheesecloth cover on the jar and sit anywhere out of the direct sun at room temperature. Let sit for about 24 hours, rinsing and draining every 8-12 hours, until small tails are forming on the quinoa.

2. Next, presoak the almonds (there is no need to soak the pistachios and chia seeds): Place the almonds into a bowl containing enough water so that they are fully immersed. Add in 1 tsp. of sea salt per every 2 c. of water to speed up the soaking process. Let the almonds soak for 8-12 hours. Be sure to change out the soaking water once or twice throughout the soaking time. When the almonds have finished soaking, rinse them thoroughly; drain. Discard the soaking water.

3. When the quinoa is ready, place it in a serving bowl along with the honey, vanilla extract, almonds, chia seeds, cinnamon, pistachios, nutmeg and raisins. Add in the desired amount of coconut or almond cream. Let set for 30 minutes, add coconut cream and then top with extra nuts and raisins. Serve immediately.

Protein Per Serving: 46g

RAW CORN, AVOCADO, AND BLACK BEAN SALAD

Total Time: 14 hours and 15 minutes (Includes 12 hours soaking time; 2 hours refrigeration time)

Servings: 4 (Serving Size: 1 salad)

Ingredients

- 2 ears fresh corn, silks and husks removed
- 1½ c. sprouted black beans, soaked and drained, rinsed in a colander until water runs clear
- 1 medium tomato, cut into ½-inch pieces
- ½ green bell pepper, finely chopped
- ¼ tsp. chili powder
- ¼ tsp. sea salt, or to taste
- 1 tbsp. fresh-squeezed lime juice
- ½ tsp. hot sauce, or to taste
- ¼-½ jalapeno pepper, seeded and finely chopped
- 1 avocado, peeled and sliced
- 4 lime wedges, to serve

Directions

1. Place the black beans in a bowl covered in water. Let soak for at least 12 hours, changing

out the water several times. Drain, rinse very well in a colander until water runs clear. Set aside until needed.

2. Remove the corn kernels from the cobs and place the kernels in a medium-sized mixing bowl.

3. Add in the black beans with the corn, along with all of the other remaining ingredients, except for the avocado and wedges of lime. Stir the salad to mix well, then cover the bowl with plastic wrap and place in the refrigerator for 2 hours to allow the flavors to meld.

4. Divide the salad among 4 salad dishes. Serve with sliced avocado and lime wedges.

Protein Per Serving: 16g

CUCUMBER-AVOCADO SOUP WITH CILANTRO

Total Time: 12 hours 15 minutes (Includes 8-12 hours soaking time)

Servings: 1 (Serving Size: 2 cups)

Ingredients

- 1 c. raw almonds, soaked and drained
- Filtered water, as needed
- 2 med. avocados, peeled, pitted, and cut into cubes
- 1 lg. cucumber, peeled, seed removed, chopped
- 5 lg. scallions, thinly sliced (incl. some green tops)
- ¼ c. fresh cilantro. chopped
- Pinch of sea salt, or to taste
- Pinch of fresh ground black pepper, or to taste
- Fresh cilantro sprigs, to garnish

Directions

1. First, presoak the almonds: Place the almonds into a bowl containing enough water so that they are fully immersed. Add in 1 tsp. of sea

salt per every 2 c. of water to speed up the soaking process. Let the almonds soak for 8-12 hours. Be sure to change out the soaking water once or twice throughout the soaking time. When the almonds have finished soaking, rinse them thoroughly; drain. Discard the soaking water.

2. After soaking, blend the almonds on low then slowly increasing speed for about 2 to 4 minutes while slowly adding 2 cups filtered water. Blend until smooth. Strain through a nut milk cloth or cheesecloth into a bowl, pressing or squeezing to extract all liquid. Then Discard solids and refrigerate liquid in a clean glass jar.

3. Prepare Soup: In a blender, combine the almond mixture, flesh from the avocados, cucumber, and scallions. Purée for about 2 minutes or until smooth. Stir in cilantro and pulse for 5 to 10 seconds.

4. Season with salt and pepper, to taste and then ladle into soup bowls and garnish with sprigs of fresh cilantro. Popular served cold, at room temperature or warmed.

Protein Per Serving: 32g

Dinners

NUTTY-VEGGIE BURGERS

Total Time: 35 hours 15 minutes (Includes 8 hours soaking time; 24 hours plus 3 hours hydrating time)

Servings: 4 (Serving Size: 1 burger patty; 1 burger bun)

Ingredients

Nutty-Veggie Burger Patties

- 2 stalks celery, chopped
- ¼ c. onion, chopped
- ½ red bell pepper, chopped
- 1 tbsp. sea salt
- 2 tbsp. dried oregano
- 1 c. sunflower seeds, soaked, drained, and ground
- 1 c. flax seeds, soaked, drained, and ground
- ½ c. purified water

Raw Veggie Burger Buns (Note: Buns need 24 hours of dehydrating time)

- 1½ c. raw carrots, chopped
- 4 c. sprouted buckwheat
- 1½ c. soaked whole flax seeds
- 1c. extra-virgin olive oil

- 2 tsp. curry powder
- 2 tsp. fresh rosemary (or 1/2 tsp dried)
- 2 tsp. fresh thyme (or 1/2 tsp dried)
- 2 clove garlic, chopped
- 2 tsp. sea salt
- sesame seeds (optional)

Directions

1. First, presoak the flax seeds, sunflower seeds, and the sesame seeds (opt. if wanted for buns): Place the flax seeds, sunflower seeds, and the sesame seeds (opt.) into separate bowls, each bowl containing enough water so that they are fully immersed. Add in 1 tsp. of sea salt per every 2 c. of water to speed up the soaking process. Let the flax seeds and sesame seeds soak for 8 hours and the sunflower seeds soak for 2 hours. Be sure to change out the soaking water once or twice throughout the soaking time. When the seeds have finished soaking, rinse them thoroughly; drain. Discard the soaking water.

2. ***Prepare the Raw Veggie Burger Buns:*** Place the chopped carrots in a food processor and process until finely diced. Add in the sprouted buckwheat, ¾ c. of the presoaked whole flax seeds, olive oil, curry powder, fresh or dried rosemary, fresh or dried thyme, chopped garlic, and sea salt. Process until the mixture turns dough-like.

3. Divide the dough and form into 4 whole buns (4 tops and 4 bottoms). Place the buns, face down, on mesh dehydrating screens. Sprinkle the 4 bun tops with sesame seeds, if using. Dehydrate at 105°F for 24 hours or until the buns are firm, yet soft. Do not allow them to dry out and become hard. When the buns are ready, prepare the burger patties.

4. ***Prepare the Nutty-Veggie Burger Patties:*** First, Process the vegetables as directed.

5. Place the sunflower seeds and the flax seeds in a food processor and process until finely ground. Then add in the celery, onion, red bell pepper, sea salt, dried oregano, and purified water; process until the mixture holds together when pressed between fingers.

6. Form the mixture into 4 patties. Place onto a dehydrating screen and dehydrate at 105°F for 3 hours or until done.

7. Serve patties on buns and serve with lettuce, tomato slices, mayonnaise, and ketchup, if desired.

Protein Per Serving:	36g

CLASSIC RAW LASAGNA

Total Time: 20 minutes

Servings: 2 (Serving Size: 1 serving -3 layers-)

Ingredients

- 1 large zucchini
- 1 large heirloom tomato
- 6 basil leaves
- 1 tbsp. extra-virgin olive oil
- pinch of sea salt, or more as needed
- 2 sprigs fresh basil, to garnish

For the Pesto

- 1 c. pistachios
- ¾ c. fresh basil, packed tight
- ¼ c. spinach, packed tight
- ¼ -1/3 c. extra-virgin olive oil
- ½ tsp. sea salt, or to taste
- Pinch of fresh ground black pepper, or to taste
- 1 small garlic clove, minced (opt.)

For the Ricotta

- 1 c. macadamia nuts
- 2 tbsp. nutritional yeast
- 1 tbsp. extra-virgin olive oil
- ¼ shallot, minced
- 1 tbsp. fresh parsley, minced

Directions

1. There is no need to soak the macadamia or pistachio nuts !

2. To begin, cut the zucchini in half and the cut of the ends. Using a mandolin, make thin slices, but not too thin, it needs to be sturdy. Lay the slices out on a sheet of parchment paper and then drizzle each slice with olive oil then sprinkle on sea salt and let marinate. Next, slice the tomato into at least 6 slices and sprinkle with salt; set aside.

3. **Prepare the Pesto:** In a food processor or blender, combine the pistachios, fresh basil, spinach, olive oil, sea salt, black pepper, and minced garlic (if using). Process until well blended, then transfer to a glass bowl; set aside until needed.

4. **Prepare the Ricotta:** In a blender or food processor, combine the macadamia nuts, yeast, olive oil, shallot, and the fresh parsley. Process until moderately smooth, adding a little water if needed to make the mixture smoother. Set aside until needed.

5. Assemble the lasagna by first laying 3 of the zucchini slices on a plate, overlapping each other by just a bit. Place a slice of tomato over the zucchini. Top the tomato with a basil leaf, a little pesto, and a little ricotta. Repeat process to form a second layer, then a third layer. Top the last layer with more pesto, more ricotta, and a sprig of basil. Finally, repeat to make 2nd serving and serve.

Protein Per Serving: 32g

CHEESY ENCHILADAS

Total Time: 11 hours 30 minutes (Includes 8 hours soaking time; 2-3 hours dehydrating time)

Servings: 2-3 (Serving Size: 2-3 enchiladas)

Ingredients

Tortillas

- 1 c. onion, chopped
- 2 c. corn kernels
- 2 c. tomatoes, chopped
- ½ c. flax seeds, soaked/drained and ground
- ¼ tsp. sea salt, or to taste
- ¼ tsp. fresh ground black pepper, or to taste

Cashew "Cheese" Sauce

- 2 c. cashews, soaked and drained
- ½ c. nutritional yeast
- 4 tbsp. miso
- 1 tsp. turmeric
- 2 garlic cloves, minced
- 1½ c. water, as needed
- Juice from 1 lemon

Taco Nut-Meat

- 2/3 c. walnuts, soaked and drained
- 2/3 c. pumpkin seeds, soaked and drained
- 2 tbsp. extra-virgin olive oil

- ¼ tsp. ground cumin, or to taste
- ¼ tsp. coriander, or to taste
- ¼ tsp. sea salt, or to taste

Salsa

- 4 tomatoes, chopped
- 1 white onion, chopped
- 2 avocados, peeled and chopped
- 2/3 c. fresh cilantro, chopped
- Juice from 1 lemon
- ¼ tsp. sea salt, or to taste
- ¼ tsp. fresh ground black pepper, or to taste

Directions

1. First, presoak the flax seeds, cashews, walnuts, and pumpkin seeds: Place the flax seeds, cashews, walnuts, and pumpkin seeds into separate bowls, each bowl containing enough water so that each are fully immersed. Add in 1 tsp. of sea salt per every 2 c. of water to speed up the soaking process. Let the flax seeds and pumpkin seeds each soak for 8 hours; let the walnuts soak for 4 hours; let the cashews soak for 2-3 hours. Be sure to change out the soaking water once or twice throughout the soaking time. When the flax seeds, cashews, walnuts, and pumpkin seeds have finished soaking, rinse them thoroughly; drain. Discard the soaking water.

2. ***Prepare the "tortillas":*** Place the onion, corn, and tomato into a food processor; process until

the mixture is mushy then add in the flax seeds, sea salt, and black pepper. Process again, until the mixture thickens. Spread the mixture into 6 large circles on dehydrate at 115°F for 2-3 hours or until they are pliable – like actual tortillas.

3. *Prepare the "cheese" sauce:* In a blender, combine all of the cheese ingredients in the order listed. Process until the mixture is smooth and creamy. Transfer the cheese sauce to a bowl and set aside until needed.

4. *Prepare the nut-meat:* In a food processor, combine all of the nut-meat ingredients. Pulse until the mixture becomes crumbly, like ground beef. Transfer to a bowl and set aside.

5. *Prepare the salsa:* Prepare the ingredients as directed, and then place them into a mixing bowl with lemon juice and sea salt and black pepper, to taste. Stir gently until combined.

6. *Assemble enchiladas:* Place 2-3 tortillas on each plate. Load each tortilla with salsa, nut-meat, and a little cheese sauce. Roll the tortillas up like you would a burrito and then cover them with more cheese sauce and the remains of your fillings. Serve and enjoy!

| **Protein Per Serving:** | 62g |

TACO SALAD DINNER

Total Time: 4 hours 5 minutes (Includes 4 hours soaking time

Servings: 4 (Serving Size: 1 salad)

Ingredients

- A large head of lettuce, shredded
- 1 lime

Walnut Taco Meat

- 2 c. walnuts, soaked and drained
- 1 tbsp. onion, minced
- 2-3 tbsp. chili powder
- 1 tsp. ground cumin
- ½ tsp. oregano
- ½ tsp. sea salt, or to taste
- pinch of cayenne pepper

Easy Guacamole

- 2 small, ripe avocados
- ½ c. tomato, diced
- 3 tbsp. red onion, diced
- Juice from ½ a lime
- Sea salt, to taste

Pico de Gallo

- 2 large tomatoes, seeded and diced
- ½ medium red onion, diced
- ¼ c. fresh cilantro, minced
- 1 tbsp. fresh-squeezed lime juice
- 1 jalapeno, seeded and minced
- Sea salt, to taste

Cashew Sour Cream

- 1 c. cashews, soaked and drained
- ½ c. water
- 2 tbsp. fresh-squeezed lemon juice
- 1 tsp. apple cider vinegar
- ½ tsp. sea salt

Directions

1. Presoak the walnuts and cashews: Place the walnuts and cashews into separate bowls containing enough water to cover with 1 tsp. sea salt. Let walnuts soak for 4 hours; cashews for 2-3. Then drain, rinse, and discard water.

2. **Prepare the Walnut Taco Meat:** Blend the walnuts in a food processor until they are broken into crumbs. Do not over process. Add in the remaining ingredients and pulse a few times until well blended. Transfer to a bowl; set aside until needed.

3. ***Prepare the Easy Guacamole:*** Mash the avocados in a small bowl until nearly smooth, then stir in the remaining ingredients until well blended. Set aside until needed.

4. ***Prepare the Pico de Gallo:*** Mix all of the ingredients together in a medium-sized bowl until well blended. Set aside until needed.

5. ***Prepare the Cashew Sour Cream:*** In a food processor, combine the cashews with ½ c. water; process until very smooth. Add in the remaining ingredients and process until well combined. Set aside until needed.

Protein Per Serving: 22g

PESTO PASTA WITH HEMP SEED

Total Time: 15 minutes

Servings: 2 (Serving Size: 2 cups)

Ingredients

Pesto

- 2-4 tbsp. extra-virgin olive oil, or more as needed
- 2-3 cloves garlic, minced
- Juice of 1 lemon
- 4-6 tbsp. hemp seeds
- 4 tbsp. nutritional yeast
- Pinch of sea salt, or to taste
- 1-2 bunches fresh basil

Pasta

- 2 c. kelp noodles, rinsed and chopped
- 1-2 large zucchini, julienned

Directions

1. There is no need to presoak the hemp seeds.

2. Prepare the Pesto: In a food processor or blender, combine the pesto ingredients until smooth. Add more olive oil if needed for

consistency. Add more salt, garlic, basil as needed for taste. Set aside until needed.

3. Rinse the kelp noodles and chop. Julienne 1-2 zucchini into noodles until you have a total of 4 cups of noodles. Place the noodles in a bowl, pour the pesto over the top and toss to coat well.

4. Divide among 2 serving plates and serve.

Protein Per Serving: g

BURRITOS WITH SPICY ZUCCHINI SAUCE

Total Time: 8 hours 20 minutes (Includes 8 hours soaking time)

Servings: 2-3 (Serving Size: 1 burrito)

Ingredients

Burrito Sauce

- ½ zucchini, more if preferred
- ¼ c. sesame seeds, soaked and drained
- Juice of 3 lemons
- Few sprigs of green onion
- 1 red bell pepper
- Spicy pepper (opt.)

Burritos

- 2-3 Large collards leaves (or leave of Bibb lettuce, if preferred)
- 1-3 green bell peppers, roughly chopped (quantity dependent on personal preference)
- 1 cucumber, roughly chopped
- 1-2 carrots, roughly chopped (quantity dependent on personal preference)
- 1-2 large tomatoes, roughly chopped (quantity dependent on personal preference)

- 1-2 avocados, peeled and roughly chopped (quantity dependent on personal preference)
- Fresh cilantro, torn to garnish
- Sprouts of choice, to garnish

Directions

1. First, presoak the sesame seeds: Place them in a bowls containing enough water so that they are fully immersed. Add in 1 tsp. of sea salt per every 2 c. of water to speed up the soaking process. Let sesame seeds soak for 8 hours. Be sure to change out the soaking water once or twice throughout the soaking time. When the seeds have finished soaking, rinse them thoroughly; drain. Discard the soaking water.

2. ***Prepare the Burrito Sauce:*** In a blender or food processor, combine all of the sauce ingredients. Process until smooth, set aside.

3. ***Prepare the Burritos***: First, roughly chop the green bell peppers, cucumber, carrots, tomatoes, and avocado.

4. To serve, lay a large collard leaf on each serving plate. Spoon some sauce over the leaf. Add the veggies and avocado and top them with cilantro and sprouts. Top with a little more sauce, if desired. Then roll up each leaf like you would a tortilla. Serve and enjoy!

Protein Per Serving: 24g

SPAGHETTI AND NUT-MEATBALLS

Total Time: 16 hours 30 minutes (Includes 12 hours soaking time; 2-4 hours dehydrating time)

Servings: 2 (Serving Size: 2 cups "noodles"; ½-1 c. marinara sauce)

Ingredients

Spaghetti

- 2-4 yellow and green zucchini, julienned
- Juice of 1 lemon

Tomato Sauce

- 2 c. cherry tomatoes
- 1 c. sun-dried tomatoes
- 1 tsp. tomato paste
- 2 dates
- 3 tbsp. extra-virgin olive oil
- 2 cloves garlic, minced
- 3 tbsp. fresh parsley
- 1 tsp. fresh oregano
- ½ - 1 c. fresh basil
- 1 tsp. Italian seasoning
- 1 tsp. sea salt

Nut-Meatballs

- 1 small red onion, chopped
- 1 bell pepper, chopped
- 2 carrots, chopped
- 1 c. burdock puree, very finely grated (or blended with water)
- 1 c. raw almonds, soaked and drained
- ½ c. sunflower seeds, soaked and drained
- ¼ c. walnuts, soaked and drained
- 2 cloves garlic, minced
- 1 stick celery, minced
- Pinch of turmeric, or to taste
- 1 tsp. cumin, or to taste
- 2 tsp. dried cilantro (or fresh cilantro, if preferred)

Directions

1. First, presoak the almonds, sunflower seeds, and the walnuts: Place the almonds, sunflower seeds, and the walnuts into separate bowls, each bowl containing enough water so that they are fully immersed. Add in 1 tsp. of sea salt per every 2 c. of water to speed up the soaking process. Let the almonds soak for 8-12 hours; let the walnuts soak for 4 hours; let sunflower seeds for 2 hours. Be sure to change out the soaking water once or twice throughout the soaking time. When the nuts/seeds have finished soaking, rinse them thoroughly; drain. Discard the soaking water.

2. Meanwhile, place the sun-dried tomatoes into a bowl of warm (not hot) water so that they are covered with the water and allow them to rehydrate for 1-2 hours while the nuts/seeds are soaking. Then remove the tomatoes from the water, but reserve the water.

3. In addition to soaking the sun-dried tomatoes, also place the dates into a separate bowl of water and let soak for 2 hours. Then remove the dates from the water; discard the water.

4. *Prepare the "Spaghetti Noodles":* Julienne the zucchini until you are left with thin spaghetti-like noodles, place the noodles in a bowl and toss with the lemon juice. Set aside until needed.

5. *Prepare the sauce:* In a blender, combine all of the sauce ingredients and process until smooth. Add in the water that the tomatoes soaked in if the sauce needs a bit of thinning. Set aside.

6. *Prepare the Nut-Meatballs:* Place all of the nut-meatball ingredients into a food processor and process until well blended, adding a bit of water, if needed.

7. Lay a sheet of parchment paper out on a countertop. Transfer the meat mixture to the parchment paper. Break off a piece of the mixture and roll it into a ball. If the mixture is too crumbly and won't hold together, instead of continuing with rolling more meatballs, place a sheet of parchment paper over the meat mixture and using a rolling pin, roll the mixture out to a ½-inch thickness. Using a small round cookie cutter or a cup with a small opening, cut out little patties. On the other hand, if the

meatballs, do hold together, continue rolling pieces of the meat mixture into balls.

8. When all of the meat mixture has been processed into balls or patties. Place the balls/patties onto non-stick dehydrator sheets and dehydrate at 115°F for 2-4 hours or until the meat mixture is set.

9. To serve, Pour the sauce and meatballs into the bowl with the noodles, toss to mix and then divide onto plates and serve!

Protein Per Serving: 41g

FISH STICKS

Total Time: 19 hours 35 minutes (Includes 8-12 hours soaking time; 5-7 hours dehydrating time)

Servings: 2-3 (Serving Size: 4-6 fish sticks)

Ingredients

"Fish Batter"

- 1 c. soaked and drained raw almonds
- 1 c. soaked and drained raw sunflower seeds
- ½ c. minced celery
- ½ c. minced red onion
- 1 tbsp. plus 1 tsp. kelp powder (for fishy flavor)
- ¼ c. fresh-squeezed lime juice
- 1 tsp. coconut aminos (or Braggs liquid aminos)
- 1 tsp. sea salt, or to taste
- 1 tsp. dried dill (or 1 tbsp. fresh)
- ½ c. water

"Breading" (yields 1¼ cups)

- ½ c. raw cashews, soaked and drained
- ¼ c. flax seeds, soaked/drained and ground
- 1 tsp. nutritional yeast
- 1 tsp. paprika (smoked)
- ½ tsp. fresh ground black pepper
- 1 tsp. sea salt

Directions

1. First, presoak the almonds, sunflower seeds, cashews, and the flax seeds: Place the each nut/seed into separate bowls, each bowl containing enough water so that they are fully immersed. Add in 1 tsp. of sea salt per every 2 c. of water to speed up the soaking process. Let the almonds soak for 8-12 hours; let the sunflower seeds soak for 2 hours; let cashews soak for 2-3 hours; let the flax seeds soak for 8 hours. Be sure to change out the soaking water once or twice throughout the soaking time. When the nuts/seeds have finished soaking, rinse them thoroughly; drain. Discard the soaking water.

2. In a food processor, ground the flax seeds. Transfer to a bowl; set aside.

3. After soaking, place the almonds and sunflower seeds in food processor until they form a paste.

4. Add in the Braggs Aminos, celery, sea salt, lime juice, onion, kelp powder, and dill. Process until mixed, stopping and scraping down the sides as needed.

5. With the motor running, slowly pour in the water; only enough to moisten the paste, and then transfer the moistened paste to a bowl.

6. ***Prepare the Breading:*** Place the cashews in food processor; process until they are broken into crumbs. Be careful to not over process.

7. Add in the paprika, salt, ground flax seeds, pepper and yeast. Pulse the processor until

combined and then pour into a rectangular or square container for dredging.

8. Measure 2 tbsp. of the "fish batter" and form into a fish stick. Then dredge through the breading mixture to coat and place on a mesh dehydrator sheet. Repeat process to form the rest of the fish sticks.

9. Dehydrate at 115°F for 5-7 hours or until warm. Don't over dehydrate them or they will get hard. Store any uneaten fish sticks in the fridge for up to 5 days.

10. Serve with a raw, nut-based tartar sauce, if desired.

| **Protein Per Serving:** | 43g |

RAW RAVIOLI WITH RED PESTO

Total Time: 4 hours 15 minutes (Includes 4 hours soaking time)

Servings: 2 (Serving Size: 6 ravioli with pesto)

Ingredients

Red Pesto

- 4 small tomatoes
- ¼ c. dried tomatoes
- 1/3 c. walnut halves, soaked and drained
- dash of raw chili powder
- 1 garlic clove, minced
- 1 tsp. fresh basil, chopped
- 1 tbsp. extra-virgin olive oil
- ¼ c. water

Ravioli

- Root celery, sliced into 24 equal-sized pieces

Directions

1. First, presoak the walnuts: Place the walnuts in a bowl with enough water so that they are fully immersed. Add in 1 tsp. of sea salt per every 2 c. of water to speed up the soaking process. Let the walnuts soak for 4 hours; change the soaking water once or twice throughout the soaking time. When the walnuts have finished soaking, rinse them thoroughly; drain. Discard the soaking water.

2. Prepare the Pesto: Place the walnuts, chili powder, basil, and garlic in a food processor; process until ground. Add in the olive oil and water; process until incorporated. Add in the chopped fresh tomatoes and the dried tomatoes; process for 5-10 seconds until a good pesto consistency is achieved. Transfer to a bowl; set aside.

3. Prepare the ravioli: Slice the root celery and cut into uniform pieces. You should end up with 24 slices to make 12 whole ravioli.

4. Arrange 6 ravioli pieces on each serving dish. Spoon the pesto over the ravioli and then cover the pesto with a 2nd piece of celery ravioli to complete the ravioli. Serve and enjoy.

Protein Per Serving: 9g

SPICY RAW CORN PIZZA

Total Time: 26 hours 35 minutes (Includes 8 hours soaking time; 10-18 hours dehydrating time)

Servings: 2 (Serving Size: 1 personal mini pizza)

Ingredients

Pizza crust

- 2½ c. raw walnuts, soaked/drained & dehydrated
- ½ c. golden flax seeds, soaked/drained & ground fine
- ¼ c. hemp seed
- 1 tsp. sea salt
- 2 c. packed and moist almond pulp
- ½-1 c. water

Spicy Corn Dip

- 2 c. organic corn kernels
- 1 c. yellow onion, chopped fine
- ½ c. red bell pepper, chopped fine
- ¼ c. green onions (both white and green sections), sliced
- 1 jalapeño, remove seeds and mince
- ½ tsp. powdered garlic
- 1 tbsp. chili sauce (siraccha)
- ½ c. raw vegan mayonnaise
- 2 tsp. fresh-squeezed lemon juice

- 1 tbsp. dried chives
- ½ tsp. sea salt
- ½ tsp. fresh ground black pepper
- 1 tsp raw honey

Pizza Toppings

- 3 c. Spicy Corn Dip (from recipe above)
- Fresh sprouts of choice
- 1-2 tomatoes, diced
- 1 large white onion, diced

Directions

1. Presoak the walnuts and flax seed (the hemp seed does not need to be soaked): Place the nuts/seeds in separate bowls. Add in just enough water to cover and 1 tsp. sea salt. Let the walnuts soak for 4 hours and the flax seeds soak for 8 hours. Then drain, rinse, and discard water. Remove walnuts after 4 hours. Place the in dehydrator at 115°F for 4 hours, then remove and set aside.

2. ***Prepare the Pizza Crust:*** Grind the flax seeds in a food processor. Transfer to a bowl; set aside. Place the walnuts in a food processor and pulse until the walnuts form a mixture similar to cornmeal. Do not over process! Add in the ground flax seed, hemp seeds, and sea salt. Pulse together until combined, and then transfer to mixing bowl.

3. Add in the almond pulp and ½ c. of the water. Using hands, mix well. If the batter is too dry and a few more tbsp. of water until the pizza

dough is moist enough to hold when pressed together. Roll the pizza dough into a large ball, break in half. Place the first half of dough on a non-stick dehydrator sheet and flatten to form a pizza base, creating a lip around the edges for the crust. Transfer the dough to the mesh sheet and place in the dehydrator. Sprinkle extra hemp seed and coarse sea salt over the top of the crust. Repeat to make the second pizza base with remaining dough. Place in dehydrator at 115°F for 10-18 hours until mostly dry, with some moisture remaining.

4. *Prepare the Spicy Corn Dip:* In a medium-sized bowl, combine the corn, jalapeño, onion, green onion, red pepper, and garlic. Stir to blend.

5. In a smaller bowl, whisk together the lemon juice, mayonnaise, siraccha sauce, chives, sea salt, black pepper, and honey. Whisk until smooth and then stir to combine into the corn mixture. Add in cilantro and toss to incorporate. Sprinkle on a pinch of cayenne pepper. Yield: 3 cups.

6. *Assemble the Pizza:* Lay out the pizza crust bases. Arrange a layer of sprouts on the bases. Spread the Spicy Corn Dip on top of the sprouts and then sprinkle each pizza with the diced tomato and onion. Slice and serve!

Protein Per Serving: 54g

VEGGIE-STYLE PIZZA

Total Time: 15 hours 45 minutes (Includes 2 hours soaking time; 12 hours dehydrating time)

Servings: 2 (Serving Size: 1 (6-inch) personal pan-sized pizza)

Ingredients

Pizza Crust

- 2 large ripe tomatoes
- 1 c. almond pulp (from almond milk)
- ½ c. young Thai coconut meat
- 1/3 c. golden flax seed meal
- 2-4 fresh basil leaves
- 1 medium shallot
- 1 tbsp. extra-virgin olive oil
- 1 clove garlic, crushed
- ½ tsp. sea salt

Tomato Sauce

- 1 large ripe tomato
- ½ red bell pepper
- ¼ c. sun-dried tomatoes
- 2 tbsp. nutritional yeast
- 1 tbsp. fresh herbs of choice (basil, parsley, oregano), minced
- 1 tbsp. extra-virgin olive oil
- 1 tbsp. onion, minced
- 1 tsp. onion powder

- 1 clove garlic, minced
- ½ tsp. sea salt, or to taste
- Pinch of fresh ground black pepper, or to taste

"Mozzarella" Cheese

- ¾ c. macadamia nuts
- 1 yellow bell pepper
- Juice of 1/2 lemon
- 2 tbsp. water
- 1 tbsp. nutritional yeast
- 1 medium shallot, sliced
- 1 clove garlic, minced
- ½ tsp. raw honey
- ½ tsp. sea salt

Toppings

- green bell pepper, sliced to yield ¾ cup
- white onion, sliced or diced to yield ¾ cup
- white button mushroom, sliced to yield ¾ cup
- fresh basil leaves, chopped to yield ¾ cup
- Any other preferred toppings, sliced, diced, or chopped to yield ¾ cup

Directions

1. There is no need to presoak macadamia nuts. Soak the sun-dried tomatoes into a bowl of warm (not hot) water so that they are covered with the water and allow them to rehydrate for 1-2 hours. Then remove the sun-dried tomatoes from the water; discard the water.

2. **Prepare the Crust:** In a blender, combine the coconut meat and 1 of the tomatoes; process until blended, then transfer contents to a food processor. Add in all of the remaining crust ingredients; process until a pliable dough-like mixture is formed. Divide the pizza dough in half and form a pizza bases that are the size of 2 (6-inch) personal pan-size pizza crusts. Place in the dehydrator and dehydrate at 115°F for 4 hours; flip the dough bases over and continue to dehydrate for an additional 6-8 hours.

3. **Prepare the Pizza Sauce:** In a food processor or blender, combine all of the sauce ingredients; process until an even and thick sauce forms. If the sauce is still too soupy, add in more nutritional yeast and onion powder. This will help to absorb the excess moisture.

4. **Prepare the "Mozzarella" Cheese:** Place all of the ingredients in a blender and process until smooth and creamy. Add additional water, if needed, to help the blending process.

5. **Prepare the Toppings:** Slice each topping ingredient to yield ¾ cup. Place the toppings in a bowl and stir in 1 tbsp. tomato sauce. Place in the dehydrator at 115°F for 30 minutes.

6. **Assemble the Pizza:** Place the pizza crusts on 2 serving plates. Spread on the pizza sauce. Add the cheese sauce. Sprinkle on the toppings. Place the pizzas in the dehydrator at 115°F to dehydrate for a final 20 minutes. Then slice the pizzas, serve, and enjoy.

| **Protein Per Serving:** | 38g |

VEGGIE-ALMOND NORI ROLLS

Total Time: 8 hours 25 minutes (Includes 8 hours soaking time)

Servings: 4 (Serving Size: 6 slices)

Ingredients

"Sushi" Filling

- 1 c. almonds, soaked and drained
- 2 c. cashews, soaked and drained
- 1 tbsp. fresh ginger, grated
- 1 clove garlic, chopped
- 3 carrots, chopped
- ¼ c. yellow onion, chopped
- ½ c. raisins
- 1 tsp. sea salt, or to taste
- 2 tbsp. extra-virgin olive oil
- 1 tbsp. fresh-squeezed lemon juice, from ½ of a lemon

Wraps

- 4 sheets nori
- 4 c. raw spinach leaves, washed and dried

Dipping Sauce (opt.)

- Coconut aminos (or Braggs liquid aminos)

Directions

1. First, presoak the almonds and cashews: Place the almonds and cashews into separate bowls, each bowl containing enough water so that they are fully immersed. Add in 1 tsp. of sea salt per every 2 c. of water to speed up the soaking process. Let the cashews soak for 2-3 hours; let the almonds soak for 8 hours. Be sure to change out the soaking water once or twice throughout the soaking time. When the nuts have finished soaking, rinse them thoroughly; drain. Discard the soaking water.

2. Prepare the "Sushi" Filling: Place the cashews and almonds in food processor. Process until they are formed into a fine powder; transfer to a bowl and set aside.

3. Next, in food processor, combine the garlic, ginger, onion, carrots, raisins, and sea salt. Process until broken down into smallish pieces. Add in the lemon juice, olive oil, powdered almonds/cashews and process until well blended.

4. Assembly the Nori Rolls: Place the nori sheets on a flat and dry surface. Arrange the dried spinach leaves on the bottom half of each sheet. Spoon ¼ c. of the filling on top of spinach along the edge that is close to you. Then roll up each of the nori sheets and cut into 6 slices with a sharp non-serrated knife. Place 6 nori slices onto each of the 4 serving plates and serve with coconut aminos (or Braggs liquid aminos) for dipping, if desired.

| **Protein Per Serving:** | 22g |

TACOS WITH "REFRIED BEANS" AND MANGO SALSA

Total Time: 39 hours 35 minutes (Includes 8 hours soaking time; 8 hours refrigeration time; 15-19 hours dehydrating time)

Servings: 10 (Serving Size: 2 tacos)

Ingredients

Taco Shells

- 2 c. golden flax seeds, soaked/drained and ground very fine
- 1 c. brown flax seeds soaked/drained and ground very fine
- 1 c. sunflower seeds, soaked and drained
- 2 tbs. minced sweet onion
- 3 tsp. minced garlic (with the skin)
- 1 tsp. chili powder
- 1 tsp. cayenne powder
- 1 tsp. cumin powder
- 2 tbs. poppy seeds
- Pinch of sea salt, or to taste

"Refried Beans"

- 1 c. sunflower seeds, soaked and drained

- 3 tbs. tahini
- 1 clove garlic (with skin attached), chopped
- 2 tsp. fresh-squeezed lemon juice
- 3 tsp. minced sweet onion
- 2 tsp. chili powder (or 1 tsp. cayenne pepper)
- 1 tsp. ground cumin
- 1-2 dates, pitted
- Pinch of sea salt, or to taste

Mad Mango Salsa

- 2 ripe mangoes, peeled, and cut into ¼-inch cubes
- 1 tbs. jalapeno, minced (opt.)
- 4 tbsp. fresh cilantro, chopped
- 2 tbsp. fresh-squeezed lime juice
- ½ tsp. sea salt, or to taste
- 1 tbsp. red onion, minced

Directions

1. First, presoak the flax seeds and sunflower seeds (there is no need to soak the poppy seeds): Place the both types of flax seeds and sunflower seeds into separate bowls, each bowl containing enough water so that they are fully immersed. Add in 1 tsp. of sea salt per every 2 c. of water to speed up the soaking process. Let the flax seeds soak for 8 hours; let sunflower seeds for 2 hours. Be sure to change out the soaking water once or twice throughout the soaking time. When the seeds have finished

soaking, rinse them thoroughly; drain. Discard the soaking water.

2. ***Prepare the Taco Shells:*** Place both types of the flax seeds in a food processor and process until they are very finely ground. Place all of the remaining taco shell ingredients in with the ground flax seed and process until smooth; adding just enough water to make it a good batter consistency. Transfer to a bowl and cover with plastic wrap. Place in the refrigerator for 8-12 hours.

3. Remove the taco shell batter from the refrigerator and spread thin layers of the batter out onto non-stick dehydrator sheets. Place the batter in the dehydrator and dehydrate at 105°F for 3-5 hours. Remove the batter from the dehydrator and use a large round cookie cutter or lid to create rounds. Place the rounds on the non-stick dehydrator sheets and dehydrate for 2 more hours. After 2 hours have passed, pick up the rounds and fold them in half to make taco shells. Place the formed taco shells back into the dehydrator, this time placing them on the dehydrator shelves ad continue dehydrating for 10-12 hours or until crisp. Yield: about 20 medium-sized taco shells

4. ***Prepare the "Refried Beans":*** Place all of the ingredients for the refried beans into a blender and process until smooth; adjust the seasonings as needed, to taste. Transfer to a bowl and set aside until needed.

5. ***Prepare the Mango Salsa:*** Prep the salsa ingredients as directed, combine in a glass bowl and stir until well blended.

6. **To Serve:** Place 2 taco shells on each plate. Spoon 1-2 tbsp., of the refried beans into the taco shells and top with the mango salsa. You can also add chopped tomatoes, chopped onion, etc. or add in a taco nut-meat if desired. Serve and enjoy!

| **Protein Per Serving:** | 24g |

Section 8: No Nuts Comforts

FRUIT SALSA

Total Time: 10 minutes

Servings: 4 (Serving Size: ½ c.)

Ingredients

- 1 c. fresh mango, diced
- 1 c. fresh strawberry, diced
- 1 c. fresh kiwi, diced
- 1 c. fresh pineapple, diced
- 1 c. fresh blackberries, quartered
- ½ c. red onion, diced
- 2 tbsp. honey
- 1 tbsp. fresh rosemary, finely chopped

Directions

1. Prepare ingredients as directed above.

2. Place the ingredients into a large mixing bowl. Stir gently until all ingredients are well combined.

3. Place in refrigerator to chill until ready to use or serve immediately. Salsa will store in refrigerator in airtight container for up to 3 days.

Protein Per Serving: 3g

EGGPLANT FRIES

Total Time: 21 hours 15 minutes

Servings: 3-4 (Serving Size: 2 c.)

Ingredients

- 2 eggplants
- ¼ c. extra-virgin olive oil
- ½ c. water
- 1 tbsp. tamari
- 1 tbsp. coconut palm sugar
- 1 tsp. smoked paprika
- ½ tsp. chipotle powder

Directions

1. To begin, peel the eggplants and slice them lengthwise into ¼-inch slices. Cut the slices into 1-inch wide "fries". Place the "fries" in a large bowl

2. In a small bowl, combine the remaining ingredients. Mix well. Pour over the "fries" in the bowl. Toss well to coat. Marinate at room temperature for 12 hours, stirring to coat every so often.

3. Place on dehydrator sheets and dehydrate at 115°F for 7-9 hours or until crispy. Then serve and enjoy!

Protein Per Serving: 4g

TOMATO KETCHUP

Total Time: 5 minutes

Servings: 16 (Serving Size: 2 tbsp.)

Ingredients

- 1 c. sun-dried tomatoes, soaked for 30 minutes
- 2 large tomatoes, chopped
- 2 tbsp. fresh garlic, minced (1-2 cloves)
- 6 dates, pitted
- ½ c. extra-virgin olive oil
- 2 tsp. sea salt, or more if needed to taste
- 2 tbsp. apple cider vinegar

Directions

1. First, soak the sun-dried tomatoes for 30 minutes, then drain. Transfer to blender or food processor.

2. Place the remaining ingredients in the order listed, into the blender or food processor, with the sun-dried tomatoes. Process until smooth. Add more sea salt, if need to taste.

3. Serve immediately or store in the refrigerator in an airtight container for up to 1 week. Yield 2 cups.

Protein Per Serving:	4g

DEHYDRATED APPLE RINGS

Total Time: 18 hours 10 minutes (includes 16-18 hours dehydrating time)

Servings: 10-12 (Serving Size: 1 cup)

Ingredients

- 10 large, firm Red Delicious and Golden Delicious Apples

Directions

1. To begin, wash and dry the apples. Remove the cores. It is your choice as to whether or not to remove the peels.

2. Using a mandolin or sharp paring knife, slice the apples into about 1/8 to 1/4 –inch-thick rounds.

3. Arrange the apple slices on to mesh dehydrator trays. Place them close together, without letting them touch. Dehydrate at 115°F for 16-18 hours or until they are dry, yet soft and slightly moist.

4. Remove the apples from the dehydrator and let them to cool to room temperature. Store in an airtight container in the pantry for up to 3 months.

Protein Per Serving: 1g

CANTALOUPE DESSERT SOUP WITH COCONUT MILK

Total Time: 1 hour 20 minutes

Servings: 4 (Serving Size: 1 cup)

Ingredients

- 3 c. cantaloupe, diced
- 1½ c. coconut milk
- 2 tbsp. raw honey
- Juice from 1 lime
- 2 – 3 fresh basil leaves, chopped
- ½ tsp. cinnamon
- ¼ tsp. ginger
- Pinch of sea salt, or to taste
- Basil leaves, for garnish (opt.)

Directions

1. Prepare ingredients as directed then combine the ingredients in the order listed together in your blender.

2. Blend on medium-high speed for 20-30 seconds or until smooth. Taste and adjust, if needed, by adding more cantaloupe, coconut

milk, cinnamon, or honey. Blend for 5-10 seconds more to fully incorporate then transfer contents to a pitcher.

3. Place in refrigerator to chill for 1 hour.

4. When ready to serve, pour into dessert bowls and garnish with fresh parsley (opt.). Always serve chilled!

Protein Per Serving: 4g

Section 9: Desserts

BANANA MAPLE WALNUT ICE CREAM

Total Time: 6-7 hours 10 minutes (Includes 4 hours soaking time; 2-3 hours freezing time)

Servings: 4 (Serving Size: ½ c.)

Ingredients

- 4 ripe bananas, frozen
- 2-3 tbsp. maple syrup
- 1 tsp. cinnamon powder
- 1 tsp. vanilla extract
- 1 tsp. raw organic vanilla bean powder
- 1/3 c. walnut pieces

Directions

1. First, presoak the walnuts: Place the walnuts in a bowl with enough water so that they are fully immersed. Add in 1 tsp. of sea salt per every 2 c. of water to speed up the soaking process. Let the walnuts soak for 4 hours; change the soaking water once or twice throughout the soaking time. When the walnuts have finished soaking, rinse them thoroughly; drain. Discard the soaking water.

2. Next, break each banana into 3 to 4 pieces.

3. In a food processor or high speed blender, combine the pieces of banana, maple syrup, cinnamon powder, vanilla extract, and the vanilla bean powder. Pulse until the mixture begins to become creamy. Pause processing to scrape down the sides of the blender as needed. Fold in the walnut pieces and stir gently to incorporate.

4. If using an ice cream maker, pour the mixture into the ice cream maker and process/freeze according to manufacturer directions.

5. If you do not own an ice cream maker, pour the mixture into an airtight container and freeze it for 2-3 hours, just as you would regular ice cream.

6. Once frozen, serve and enjoy! Yield: 2 cups.

| **Protein Per Serving:** | 12g |

KEY LIME PIE

Total Time: 22 hours 25 minutes (Includes 12 hour dehydrating time; 4-6 hours soaking time; 3-4 hours refrigerated time)

Servings: 8 (Serving Size: 1 slice of pie)

Ingredients

Crust Ingredients

- 1½ c. raw macadamia nuts
- 1 c. raw pecans
- ¼ c. packed Medjool dates, pitted
- 1 tbsp. lime zest, (grated peel)
- ½ tsp. cinnamon powder
- 1/8 tsp. sea salt

Filling Ingredients

- 1½ c. coconut milk (or make your own by blending meat and liquid from a fresh young coconut)
- 1/3 c. mashed ripe avocado
- 1 c. raw honey
- ¾ c. fresh-squeezed lime juice (from 3-5 limes, depending on size)
- ¼ c. fresh-squeezed lemon juice (from 1-2 lemons, depending on size)

- 3 tbsp. lecithin powder
- ¼ tsp. sea salt
- 1 c. raw coconut oil, warm very gently to liquefy

Topping Ingredients

- 1½ c. raw coconut milk (or make your own by blending meat and liquid from a fresh young coconut)
- ½ c. Thai coconut meat (from a fresh coconut – cracked and scrape meat)
- ½ c. honey
- ¼ c. Irish Moss (or agar agar, or another raw gelatin thickener)
- 1 tsp. vanilla powder or extract
- 2 tbsp. lecithin powder
- ¼ tsp. sea salt
- ½ c. coconut oil, melted
- 2 limes, sliced, to garnish
- ¼ c. reserved crust, to garnish

Directions

1. First, presoak the pecans (there is no need to soak the macadamia nuts!): Place the pecans into a bowl containing enough water so that they are fully immersed. Add in 1 tsp. of sea salt per every 2 c. of water to speed up the soaking process. Let the pecans soak for 4-6 hours. Be sure to change out the soaking water once or twice throughout the soaking time. When the pecans have finished soaking, rinse

them thoroughly; drain. Discard the soaking water.

2. Place the pecans on dehydrating sheets and dehydrate at 115°F for 12 hours or until dried and crisp.

3. **Prepare the Crust:** Place the presoaked and dehydrated macadamia nuts, pecans, cinnamon and sea salt into food processor and process until the contents turn into a crumbly meal. Add in the dates; process until the mixture is loose, but holds together when pressed between your fingertips. Be sure to not over process the ingredients, as the oil will separate.

4. Add in the lime zest and pulse until just combined. Measure out ¼ c. of crust and put aside until needed. Press the remaining crust into a 9-inch deep glass pie dish and set aside until needed.

5. **Prepare the Filling:** Place the avocado with the coconut milk into the blender with the lime juice, honey, and sea salt; process until smooth. While the motor is running, add in the lecithin with the melted coconut oil and continue processing until smooth.

6. Pour the filling mixture over the surface of crust in the pie dish. Smooth out the top of the filling with a rubber spatula or gently tap the pie dish on the counter a couple of time to smooth out the surface of the filling. Place the pie in the refrigerator to chill for at least 3 hours - until firm. When the pie filling is firm, prepare the topping.

7. ***Prepare the Topping:*** Place all of the topping ingredients, minus the lecithin, coconut oil, and slices of lime, into the blender; process until smooth. With the motor still running, add in the lecithin and melted coconut oil; continue processing until smooth and creamy.

8. Pour topping onto the firm (chilled) pie filling. Smooth the surface of the topping with a rubber spatula or knife. Then slice and serve, garnishing each slice with a little of the reserved ¼ c. of extra crust and 1-2 slices of lime, if desired.

| **Protein Per Serving:** | 23g |

CHOCOLATE CHIP MINT ICE CREAM

Total Time: 5 minutes (Includes 8 hours soaking time and 2-3 hours of freezing time)

Servings: 4 (Serving Size: ½ cup)

Ingredients

- 2 c. almond milk , see recipe below
- 2 c. coconut meat from a fresh, young Thai coconut
- 1/3 c. coconut palm sugar
- 1 tbsp. maple syrup
- 1 tbsp. raw honey
- 2 tsp. vanilla extract (or1 vanilla bean pod, scraped)
- 2 tbsp. coconut oil
- ¼ tsp. sea salt
- 1 c. fresh mint leaves, stems removed
- Pinch of spirulina, or more as needed for "green" coloring of ice cream (opt.)
- ½-1c. raw organic chocolate chips (or cacao nibs, if preferred)

Almond Milk

- 1 c. raw almonds, soaked and drained

- 1½ c. water, or more as needed for desired consistency
- 1-6 Medjool dates, pitted (quantity depending on personal taste preference
- 1 tsp. vanilla extract

Directions

1. First, presoak the almonds: Place them in a bowl with enough water that they are fully immersed. Add in 1 tsp. of sea salt per every 2 c. of water to speed up the soaking process. Let the almonds soak for 8 hours; change the soaking water once or twice throughout the soaking time. When the almonds have finished soaking, rinse them thoroughly; drain. Discard the soaking water. When the almonds are ready, prepare the almond milk.

2. ***Prepare the almond milk:*** In a blender, combine the almonds and 1½ c. water. Process until well blended.

3. Strain the blended mixture through a fine wire mesh strainer or a nut milk bag. Using a spoon or spatula, help push the milk strain through the nut meal. Then return mixture to the blender and add in 1-2 pitted dates and the vanilla extract. Process until smooth. Taste; add more dates, if desired for taste. Add more water, if desired to reach your preferred consistency. Process until smooth. Measure out 2 cups of the almond milk for the ice cream and store any

remaining almond milk in a glass jar with lid in the refrigerator for 5-7 days.

4. ***Prepare the Chocolate Chip Mint Ice Cream:***
In a blender, combine the almond milk, coconut meat, coconut palm sugar, maple syrup, honey, vanilla extract (or scraped vanilla bean pod), coconut oil, sea salt, and fresh mint. Process for 3 minutes or until the mixture is smooth and creamy. If you want the ice cream to be more green in color, add in pinch at a time of spirulina, blending to incorporate after each addition, until desired color is achieved. Just do not add too much, because it could end up altering the flavor of the ice cream.

5. If using an ice cream maker, first place the ice cream in an airtight container and place in the freezer for 1 hour, then pour the mixture into the ice cream maker and process/freeze according to manufacturer directions.

6. If you do not own an ice cream maker, pour the mixture into an airtight container and freeze it for 2-3 hours, stirring a few times per hour, until frozen.

7. Finally, just when the ice cream is about to freeze, fold in chocolate chips (or cacao nibs).

8. Once frozen, serve and enjoy! Yield: 2 cups.

Protein Per Serving: 44g

KEFIR (FERMENTED) CHEESECAKE (NOT VEGAN)

Total Time: 4 days 12 hours 35 minutes (8 hours soaking time; 4 hours dehydrating time; 4 days fermenting time; 3-4 hours refrigeration time)

Servings: 8-10 (Serving Size: 1 slice)

Ingredients

Crust

- ¾ c. almonds, soaked and drained
- ½ c. pecans, soaked and drained
- ¾ c. Californian dates

Kefir

- ¼ c. kefir grains
- 3 c. raw milk, from organic pasture fed cows

Kefir Cream

- ½ c. of the prepared fermented kefir
- 1½ c. raw double-weight cream

Filling

- ¾ c. raw milk, from organic pasture fed cows
- 1-2 tbsp. raw coconut butter (or coconut oil), softened
- 1 tbsp. gelatin
- 2 c. of the prepared fermented kefir cream
- ¼ c. raw honey
- 2 large eggs, yolks and whites separated
- ¼ tsp. vanilla extract
- 2 tsp. lime juice or lemon juice
- Pinch of sea salt, or as needed to taste

Directions

1. First, presoak the pecans and almonds: Place the pecans and almonds into separate bowls, each bowl containing enough water so that they are fully immersed. Add in 1 tsp. of sea salt per every 2 c. of water to speed up the soaking process. Let the pecans soak for 4-6 hours; let the almonds soak for 8 hours. Be sure to change out the soaking water once or twice throughout the soaking time. When the pecans and almonds have finished soaking, rinse them thoroughly; drain. Discard the soaking water. Set the cashews aside until needed. Dry the almonds by placing them in the dehydrator at 115°F for about 4 hours, turning the almonds a couple times per hour, until dry.

2. Prepare the Kefir: To prepare the kefir, combine the ¼ c. kefir grains with the 3 c. raw milk and let ferment at room temperature for 12-24 hours, and then transfer to the refrigerator until

ready to use. Be sure to remove the kefir grains from the kefir before preparing the Kefir Cream.

3. Prepare the Kefir Cream: When kefir is finished, combine the ½ c. of the fermented kefir with 1½ c. double-weight cream. Let ferment at room temperature for 12-24 hours. Then transfer to the refrigerator until ready to use.

4. Preparing and Assembling the Cheesecake: Place the cashews and almonds into a blender or food processor and process until they are ground as finely as possible. Chop the dates and then add them to the blender or food processor with the ground nuts. Process until well blended.

5. Grease a flat cake tray or dish with the softened coconut butter (or coconut oil). Press the nut-date crust mixture onto the tray/dish with your fingers (use the bottom of a glass, if needed) to form a thin crust.

6. Place the milk in a saucepan and use a candy thermometer to ensure the temperature stays below 115°F. Sprinkle the gelatin into the milk and let warm slightly, and beat with a wire whisk or large fork until dissolved. Sit the saucepan into a bowl of cool water to cool the milk mixture to body temperature.

7. In your food processor or blender, combine the egg yolks, raw honey, kefir cream, vanilla and lime (or lemon) juice; process at medium-low speed for up to 30 seconds, until smooth. Make sure the honey is blended into the mixture and is not stuck at the bottom. Set the custard mixture aside.

8. In a separate bowl, beat the egg whites (and a pinch of salt) together until small peaks are formed. Set aside.

9. Working quickly, combine in the blender, the milk mixture (cooled) and the custard mixture. Process at low to medium for up to 30 seconds or until smooth. Transfer mixture to a bowl then carefully fold in egg whites with your spatula.

10. Pour mixture into crust and place in refrigerator for at least 3 hours before serving.

Protein Per Serving: 39g

RAW PEACH COBBLER

Total Time: 12 hours 10 minutes (8-12 hours soaking time)

Servings: 2 (Serving Size: 1 peach cobbler dessert)

Ingredients

- 2½ c. peaches, pitted and sliced
- 5-6 medjool dates, pitted
- 1 c. raw coconut meat or flakes
- ½ c. almonds, soaked and drained
- 1 tsp. vanilla extract
- 3 tbsp. raw honey
- 3 tbsp. coconut oil

Directions

1. First, presoak the almonds: Place the almonds into a bowl containing enough water so that they are fully immersed. Add in 1 tsp. of sea salt per every 2 c. of water to speed up the soaking process. Let the almonds soak for 8-12 hours. Be sure to change out the soaking water once or twice throughout the soaking time. When the pecans and almonds have finished

soaking, rinse them thoroughly; drain. Discard the soaking water.

2. Slice and pit peaches; set aside.

3. In a food processor, combine the dates, coconut, almonds and a pinch sea salt; process until sticky and blended. Set aside.

4. In a blender, combine ½ cup of peaches with the vanilla extract, honey, and coconut oil; process until smooth.

5. To serve, place 1 sliced peach in each bowl, pour the peach-vanilla sauce over the peaches and then sprinkle on the "cobbler" (the almond-date mixture) over each serving and serve immediately.

Protein Per Serving: 11g

VANILLA BEAN ICE CREAM

Total Time: 4-6 hours 10 minutes (includes 2-3 hours soaking time; 2-3 hours freezing time)

Servings: 4 (Serving Size: ½ c.)

Ingredients

- 2 vanilla beans
- 2 cups cashews, coarsely chopped
- 2 cups purified water
- 1 cup maple syrup

Directions

1. First, presoak the cashews: Place them in a bowl with enough water that they are fully immersed. Add in 1 tsp. of sea salt per every 2 c. of water to speed up the soaking process. Let the cashews soak for 2-3 hours; change the soaking water once or twice throughout the soaking time. When the cashews have finished soaking, rinse them thoroughly; drain. Discard the soaking water.

2. Place the vanilla beans into a food processor and process until finely ground. Transfer the ground vanilla to a blender.

3. Place the coarsely chopped cashews, purified water, and maple syrup into the blender. Process until well combined.

4. If using an ice cream maker, pour the mixture into the ice cream maker and process/freeze according to manufacturer directions.

5. If you do not own an ice cream maker, pour the mixture into an airtight container and freeze it for 2-3 hours, just as you would regular ice cream.

6. Once frozen, serve and enjoy! Yield: 2 c.

Protein Per Serving: 10g

DOODH PEDHA

Total Time: 3 hours 10 minutes (Includes 2-3 hours soaking time)

Servings: 6-8 (Serving Size: 2 pieces)

Ingredients

- 1 c. cashews, soaked and drained
- ¾ c. coconut flour
- 2 tbsp. turbinado sugar (or coconut palm sugar)
- 2 tsp. cardamom powder
- 2-3 tsp. rose water
- 1 tsp. saffron powder

Directions

1. First, presoak the cashews: Place the cashews in a bowl with enough water so that they are fully immersed. Add in 1 tsp. of sea salt per every 2 c. of water to speed up the soaking process. Let the cashews soak for 2-3 hours; change the soaking water once or twice throughout the soaking time. When the cashews have finished soaking, rinse them thoroughly; drain. Discard the soaking water.

2. Place all of the ingredients into a blender; process until a well-blended dough forms.

3. Using your hands, break off 1 tbsp. size of dough and roll into a ball. Repeat until all dough is used.

4. You can press small frit pieces into the center of the balls of dough to decorate, if desired.

5. Serve right away or store in the refrigerator in an airtight container for about 1 week.

Protein Per Serving: 8g

CHOCOLATE CHIP COOKIES

Total Time: 16 hours 25 minutes (Includes 4 hours soaking time; 10-12 hours dehydrating time)

Servings: 4 (Serving Size: 8 fl.oz.)

Ingredients

- 2 c. raw rolled oats
- 1 c. raw flaked oats, ground to yield 1 c. oat flour
- 1 c. unsweetened flaked coconut
- 1 tsp. sea salt
- 1 c. raw cashew (or almond) nut butter
- ½ c. coconut palm sugar
- ¼ c. raw honey
- 1½ tsp. vanilla extract
- ¼ c. raw coconut oil, melted
- 1 c. walnuts, soaked/drained and roughly chopped.
- 1-2 c. raw chocolate chips (or cacao nibs)

Directions

1. First, presoak the walnuts. Place them in a bowl with enough water to cover and add in 1 tsp. sea salt. Soak for 4 hours, then rinse the walnuts, drain, and discard the soaking water.

Dry the walnuts with paper towel and then roughly chop. Set aside until needed.

2. Place 1 c. of the raw oats into a food processor and process until a fine oat flour forms. Leave the oat flour in the processor and add in the raw flaked oats and the sea salt. Pulse 2 quick bursts to just combine. Then add in the raw nut butter, coconut palm sugar, honey, and vanilla extract. Process until well blended. With the motor still running, gradually pour in the melted coconut oil. Process until a nice even, textured dough forms.

3. Transfer the cookie dough to a large mixing bowl. Using a wooden spoon, gently fold in the flaked coconut, chopped walnuts, and chocolate chips (or cacao nibs) until incorporated.

4. Break of a piece of the dough that is about the size of a heaping tbsp. Using your hands, roll it into a ball, place on a mesh dehydrator sheet and use the back of a spoon to slightly flatten. Repeat with remaining dough. You should end up with about 34 cookies.

5. Place the cookies in the dehydrator and dehydrate at 115°F for 10-12 hours or until dry, yet soft. Serve right away. Store cookies in the refrigerator in an airtight container for 1-2 wccks or freeze them to store for at least 1 month.

Protein Per Serving: 26g

PECAN SANDIES

Total Time: 18 -24 hours and 20 minutes (Includes 4-6 hours soaking time and 12-24 hours dehydrating time)

Servings: 12 (Serving Size: 2 cookies)

Ingredients

- 3 c. raw pecans, presoaked and drained (to yield 1 ½ c. ground pecans and 24 whole pecan halves)

Pecan Sandies

- 1¾ c. dried unsweetened flaked coconut
- 1½ c. pecans, ground
- ¾ c. maple syrup
- 1/3 c. coconut oil, softened
- 1 tsp. vanilla extract (or 1 vanilla bean, scraped, if preferred)
- 1 tsp. almond extract (opt.)
- Dash of sea salt
- 24 pecan halves

Directions

1. First, presoak the pecans: Place the pecans in a bowl with enough water so that they are fully immersed. Add in 1 tsp. of sea salt per every 2 c. of water to speed up the soaking process. Let the pecans soak for 4-6 hours; change the soaking water once or twice throughout the soaking time. When the pecans have finished

soaking, rinse them thoroughly; drain. Discard the soaking water. Take out 24 pecan halves, set them aside until needed. Take the rest of the pecans and place them in a food processor. Pulse until they are ground and measure out 1½ c. of the ground pecans and set aside until needed.

2. In a large mixing bowl combine, flaked coconut, 1½ c. ground pecans, maple syrup, softened coconut oil, vanilla extract (or scraped vanilla bean), almond extract (opt.), and a pinch of sea salt. Mix until well combined.

3. Take 1 tbsp. of the mixture into your hand and form it into a ball, place the ball of dough onto a non-stick dehydrator sheet, and press down and flatten slightly with the back of a tablespoon. Press 1 of the pecan halves in the center of the flattened ball and press it lightly into the dough. Repeat with remaining dough and pecan halves to make the remaining 23 cookies. Use multiple non-stick dehydrating sheets, if needed.

4. Dehydrate the pecan sandies at 115°F for 12-24 hours or until done. Yield: 24 Pecan Sandies.

| **Protein Per Serving:** | 12g |

CHOCOLATE ICE CREAM

Total Time: 4-6 hours 10 minutes (includes 2-3 hours soaking time; 2-3 hours freezing time)

Servings: 4 (Serving Size: ½ c.)

Ingredients

- 1¾ c. cashews, coarsely chopped
- 1¾ c. purified water
- 1 c. maple syrup
- 2 tsp. vanilla extract
- ¼ tsp. almond extract
- ½ c. unsweetened cocoa powder

Directions

1. First, presoak the cashews: Place them in a bowl with enough water that they are fully immersed. Add in 1 tsp. of sea salt per every 2 c. of water to speed up the soaking process. Let the cashews soak for 2-3 hours; change the soaking water once or twice throughout the soaking time. When the cashews have finished soaking, rinse them thoroughly; drain. Discard the soaking water.

2. In a blender, combine the coarsely chopped cashews, purified water, maple syrup, vanilla extract, almond extract, and cocoa powder. Process until well combined.

3. If using an ice cream maker, pour the mixture into the ice cream maker and process/freeze according to manufacturer directions.

4. If you do not own an ice cream maker, pour the mixture into an airtight container and freeze it for 2-3 hours, just as you would regular ice cream.

5. Once frozen, serve and enjoy! Yield: 2 cups.

Protein Per Serving: 10g

Jon Symons

Keep in Touch

If you have any questions or comments, contact me at jon@jonsymons.com or at my blog JonSymons.com, I'm very happy to hear from you and help out any way I can. You can see all of my books on my Amazon Author page: http://bit.ly/jon-symons-amazon

If you haven't done it yet, make sure to grab your bonus eBook that I wrote which is a perfect companion to this book: Easy Small Sprouts (http://bit.ly/sprouting-guide).

And lastly, if you would be so kind as to take a moment and leave a review for this book on Amazon, that would be very much appreciated. Even 2 or 3 words and an honest rating would help other readers find my books: http://jonsymons.com/raw-food-protein-review/

Printed in Great Britain
by Amazon.co.uk, Ltd.,
Marston Gate.